The Other Jersey Shore

Also by Michael Aaron Rockland

Nonfiction/Scholarship

Sarmiento's Travels in the United States in 1847
America in the Fifties and Sixties: Julián Marías on the United States (editor)
The American Jewish Experience in Literature
Homes on Wheels
Looking for America on the New Jersey Turnpike (coauthored with Angus Kress
    Gillespie)
What's American About American Things?
Popular Culture: Or Why Study "Trash"?
The Jews of New Jersey: A Pictorial History (coauthored with Patricia Ard)
The George Washington Bridge: Poetry in Steel

Nonfiction Memoir

Snowshoeing Through Sewers
An American Diplomat in Franco Spain
Navy Crazy

Fiction

A Bliss Case
Stones
Married to Hitler

Screenplay

Three Days on Big City Waters (coauthored with Charles Woolfolk)

The Other Jersey Shore

Life on the Delaware River

MICHAEL AARON ROCKLAND

Rutgers University Press

New Brunswick, Camden, and Newark, New Jersey

London and Oxford

Rutgers University Press is a department of Rutgers, The State University of New Jersey, one of the leading public research universities in the nation. By publishing worldwide, it furthers the University's mission of dedication to excellence in teaching, scholarship, research, and clinical care.

Library of Congress Cataloging-in-Publication Data

Names: Rockland, Michael Aaron, author.
Title: The other Jersey shore : life on the Delaware river / Michael Aaron Rockland.
Other titles: Life on the Delaware river
Description: New Brunswick, New Jersey : Rutgers University Press, [2024] | Includes bibliographical references and index.
Identifiers: LCCN 2023044030 | ISBN 9781978828384 (paperback) | ISBN 9781978828391 (cloth) | ISBN 9781978828407 (epub) | ISBN 9781978828414 (pdf)
Subjects: LCSH: Delaware River (N.Y.-Del. and N.J.)—Description and travel. | Delaware River (N.Y.-Del. and N.J.)—History. | Delaware Bay (Del. and N.J.)—Description and travel. | Delaware Bay (Del. and N.J.)—History. | New Jersey—History, Local. | BISAC: NATURE / Ecosystems & Habitats / Rivers | TRAVEL / Special Interest / Ecotourism
Classification: LCC F142.D4 R63 2024 | DDC 974.9—dc23/eng/20231108
LC record available at https://lccn.loc.gov/2023044030

A British Cataloging-in-Publication record for this book is available from the British Library.

Photos by the author unless otherwise indicated

References to internet websites (URLs) were accurate at the time of writing. Neither the author nor Rutgers University Press is responsible for URLs that may have expired or changed since the manuscript was prepared.

⊗ The paper used in this publication meets the requirements of the American National Standard for Information Sciences—Permanence of Paper for Printed Library Materials, ANSI Z39.48-1992.

rutgersuniversitypress.org

For Jude and Alexa, and Jett and Romi,
who are even more beautiful than the river

A river is more than an amenity,
it is a treasure.

OLIVER WENDELL HOLMES

A river is flowing in and through you
carrying the message of joy.

SRI CHINMOY

Contents

Foreword

On a map the Delaware River and Bay may look like dividing lines that separate communities in New York, New Jersey, Pennsylvania, and Delaware. In reality, on the ground and on the water, the river and bay are connectors, bringing communities together to enjoy the beauty of nature and to benefit from the many values that healthy, natural waterways and landscapes provide. In his consideration of the Delaware, Michael Aaron Rockland so beautifully captures the truth that there is no aspect of life in this region that is not touched by the river—its quality, ecosystems, and landscapes. Whether looking at the river's role in our region's history or examining its influence on our lives today, we see that when the river is in decline the people and our communities are harmed. When the river is vibrant, cared for, protected, and healthy, our people and communities thrive.

Too often when people hear about the "Jersey Shore," they automatically think of beaches such as those at Atlantic City, Cape May, Avalon, Mantoloking, and Wildwood. In this book, Rockland captures the magic and majesty of the New Jersey landscapes and waters of the Delaware River and Bay, the "Other Jersey Shore" of his title. Rockland takes the reader on a journey from the river's pristine upper reaches where communities fish, canoe, and swim to the sandy shores of Delaware Bay with its quiet and all but abandoned beaches, which provide a different kind of experience than the crowded Atlantic beaches. The diversity of the 331 miles of the Delaware—its people, landscapes, and towns—is celebrated throughout the book.

The river also supports a unique combination of biodiversity and natural ecosystems. Among the most renowned and spectacular sights is the spring arrival of the migratory shorebirds—so many they can blacken the sky as they swoop in to feast on the energy-rich eggs of the Delaware Bay's horseshoe crab population, the largest in the world. People travel from near and far to witness and enjoy this natural spectacle.

The Delaware is a river filled with life, both in its waters and along its banks. As Rockland recounts, this beautiful and diverse use of every part of the river's system is not a new phenomenon. It has characterized the entire history of the river system from its pre-Columbian uses by the Leni Lenape to modern life.

In the air, herons and raptors, such as a rapidly restoring population of eagles, use the river to guide their annual flights to breeding grounds and overwintering sites and to search for food and the resting spots that support the many facets of their life cycles. The river also helps guide fish on yearly migrations from the ocean upriver to spawn in their natal waters. Hundreds of aquatic species rely on the river, which supports both commercial and recreational fishing, but there are some species precious to the water that are not doing well. Among those in radical decline is a genetically unique population of Atlantic sturgeon that only spawns in the Delaware River and Bay and has been seriously damaged from decades of abuse—female 800-pound fish killed only to harvest their eggs or caviar.

Whether we are talking about tributary streams or the wide waters of the bay, the forests of the Kittatinny Ridge or the urban landscapes of Philadelphia and Camden, the watershed's abundant species or its endangered ones, there is something about the Delaware River that gets under your skin, that changes you. And because of that, the region is also home to a host of powerful and caring advocates who have been touched by its waters, lands, and diversity of life. These advocates now prioritize the restoration and protection of a healthy Delaware River. Their efforts—those of our Delaware Riverkeeper Network among them—are not only so that all people and species can benefit from the joy and bounty that our river provides but also to ensure that this joy and bounty of our river and watershed, and its wider effects on our nation and planet, endure for generations yet to come.

When reading *The Other Jersey Shore*, you will become inspired by Michael Aaron Rockland to become one of the vigilant and unyielding advocates that our river and its communities need and deserve.

Maya K. van Rossum is the Delaware Riverkeeper and leader of the Delaware Riverkeeper Network. She is the author of The Green Amendment: The People's Fight for a Clean, Safe, and Healthy Environment.

The Other Jersey Shore

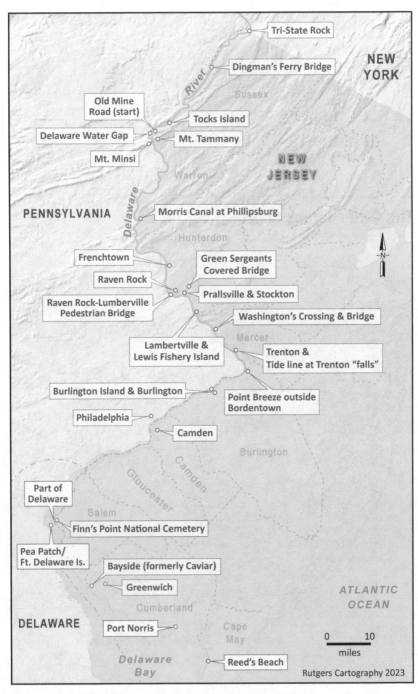

This map of New Jersey indicates the key sites discussed in the book. Rutgers Cartography 2023.

Introduction

Given that *The Other Jersey Shore* is the title of this book, I should begin by mentioning what this book does not focus on, what shore it is not about. It is not about the town of Jersey Shore, Pennsylvania, located some fifteen miles southwest of Williamsport on the west bank of the Susquehanna River. That Jersey Shore was first inhabited by some New Jerseyans who had relocated there in the late eighteenth century and found themselves in a rivalry with neighbors across the river who, when they referred to "those Jersey Shore people," meant the people on the other side of the river and meant it pejoratively. As the number of people on the other side of the river grew, what had been a putdown became in 1826 the official name of a town, Jersey Shore, and it has been ever since (population today, 4,200). Many are the people, including this author, who drive through Pennsylvania and, upon seeing the signs for Jersey Shore, wonder if they are hopelessly lost. I have talked with people in Jersey Shore, Pennsylvania. Almost universally, they find nothing peculiar about their town's name. They have, for generations, been so accustomed to living with it that they shrug and simply say, "That's the name of our town." One young man even said to me, quite irately, as if I was criticizing his town's name, "What's your problem?"

This book is also not a behind-the-scenes look at a certain infamous, at least to my taste, television show of some years back called *Jersey Shore* or meant to present that show in an alternate light suggested by the word "other." It is currently rumored that now, several years since human civilization, and New Jersey's in particular, was rescued by the closing of the show, *Jersey Shore 2.0* is being proposed. In any case, this book does not concern itself with it or its predecessor—since they represent in an extreme form values and attitudes foreign to the Jersey shore I wish to celebrate.

It goes without saying that this book is obviously not about what most people in New Jersey and neighboring states think of as the Jersey Shore—those 127 miles of sand and 44 beaches extending from Sandy Hook to Cape May. Nor does the book argue for a new way of regarding that shore.

Instead, it is concerned with an entirely different Jersey shore with which the state is blessed, the one on the west side of the state, less known and relatively ignored: the shore of the Delaware River.

There have been hundreds of books about the beaches on the Atlantic shore, and many millions have experienced it, but little is known by the average person about the Jersey shore of the Delaware River. For example, an otherwise world-traveled friend of mine, learning that I was writing this book, asked, "Is the Delaware that river I cross to get to Pennsylvania?" That seemed to be all he knew of the river and the culture of its shore.

Another person with whom I was engaged in conversation about this book said, "Isn't that the river George Washington crossed to attack Trenton?" He was partially right, but that seemed to be the limit of his knowledge or experience of the Delaware.

One reason for this ignorance about the Delaware and its Jersey shore is its lack of media attention. For example, there is a book of photographs titled *New Jersey: An American Portrait* that has a whole section on the Atlantic beaches but not a single picture of the Delaware River or of the state's prettiest towns that line its banks[1]—not even a picture of the Delaware Water Gap, which appears on some lists of the Eight Wonders of the World and may soon be declared part of a national park, the first in our area of the country.

Is there anything remotely the Gap's equal on the Atlantic side of the state? While I will consider the highlights of the river on its Jersey banks, I must admit to an ulterior purpose: demonstrating that New Jersey's Delaware shore is both more beautiful and at least as, if not more, cloaked in history as its better-known counterpart. I should acknowledge that my judgement is probably clouded by being more a lover of rivers and mountains and trees than sandy beaches. I guess I prefer the smell of pine trees to that of rancid suntan lotion and scorched flesh. Nevertheless, I should acknowledge that the beaches collaborate with the Delaware in defeating the stereotype of the Garden State engendered by the Turnpike and some of its miserable, albeit dramatic, northern surroundings.

But calling New Jersey the Garden State may be a gross exaggeration, if not a misnomer. Indeed, when this nickname was proposed by legislation in the 1950s it was vetoed by Governor Robert Meyner, who thought it did not represent the state appropriately, though his veto was overcome by the legislature. Meyner felt "Garden State" would invite derision because New Jersey was not particularly garden-like, but largely industrial, technological, and the most densely populated of the fifty states. Indeed, it did invite derision. Truckdrivers entering New Jersey have routinely referred to it on their CB radios not as the Garden State but as the "Garbage State," and the television program *Saturday Night Live* and Woody Allen movies have often had a field day at New Jersey's expense. It may not be "the armpit of the universe," as John Belushi regularly referred to it in the early days of *Saturday Night Live*, but it's not the Garden of Eden and should not be called the Garden State. If I had my way, I'd call it the Bill of Rights State, since New Jersey was the first to endorse the first ten amendments to the Constitution. That's something praiseworthy and accurate that might be celebrated on automobile license plates and elsewhere, just as Connecticut and Delaware celebrate similar distinctions on their license plates.

But there is still plenty of "garden" in New Jersey (using the term liberally to mean natural beauty) and the nicest part of it is along the Delaware River. This book means to take you there.

The Joy of a River

American landscape paintings invariably feature a beautiful river. I can't recall a painting by George Inness without one. Or Thomas Cole. And in these, unlike in paintings of European landscapes, one sees almost no signs of civilization—a house, a church, people—nothing but the river itself. In Cole's 1836 *The Oxbow* (of the Connecticut River) one would have to look at length to see that, virtually lost in an immense natural scene, close by the river, is a tiny figure with an umbrella and what appears to be an easel; it is likely Cole himself at work painting this very picture.

In most European landscape painting the occasional appearance of a river is usually incidental, the background of a social scene. An example would be the French painter Georges Seurat's celebrated pointillist painting, *A Sunday Afternoon on the Island of La Grande Jatte*, where crowds of people, his true subject, dominate the picture, the River Seine in the background and of little consequence. In typical American landscape painting the river *is* the subject. It also invariably does not appear restricted to either side of the painting but suggests that it is entering from beyond the frame on one end and continuing beyond it on the other. It gives the impression that the river is flowing through the painting.

American and European attitudes toward nature tend to differ, Americans, with some exceptions, preferring nature wild, Europeans cultivated. American gardeners are generally interested in giving the impression, despite considerable personal labor, that their gardens grew by themselves, are "natural." Think, in contrast, of a manicured Italian formal garden. Such a garden is often as carefully arranged as the furniture inside a house or palace, if not more so. Asher B. Durand's 1849 painting *Kindred Spirits* expresses well the American view. Thomas Cole and the nature poet William Cullen Bryant stand on a rocky ledge overlooking a deep gorge and a raging river and waterfall. Cole and Bryant were kindred spirits in their friendship and shared interests, but the deeper meaning of the painting's title is the kinship the men feel with their natural surroundings. For most Americans, people are part of nature, not separate and divorced from it.

As for the Delaware, there is, in addition to its wild beauty, the history that has taken place on its banks. Not that the Atlantic Jersey shore is absent all history. Seven presidents vacationed there, mostly in Long Branch: Grant, Benjamin Harrison, Hayes, Arthur, McKinley, Wilson, and Nixon. There is a public beach in Long Branch known as Seven Presidents Beach. President Garfield also went to Long Branch, not to vacation but in an unsuccessful attempt to recover from an assassin's bullet. But except for the death of a president, history was not much made on the Atlantic Jersey shore.

As an example of history on the Delaware, George Washington and his ragtag army crossed it not once but four times, leading to the victories that gave America hope, after a multitude of defeats, that it might yet win its independence. If, as historians have argued, New Jersey was "the cockpit" of the Revolutionary War, these several crossings of the Delaware, and the two (Yes, two!) Battles of Trenton and the Battle of Princeton that followed, may be seen as when that expression first took on meaning.

Another remarkable piece of history that characterizes the Delaware is the residence for the better part of twenty years of Napoleon's brother Joseph there, following his years as the appointed (by his brother) King of Spain. It was on a bluff overlooking the Delaware on the outskirts of Bordentown, New Jersey. He built a huge mansion, rivaling the White House in size and grandeur, and, when that burned down, built another. Besides the key battles and residence of Joseph Bonaparte, there would be more than enough material to write a book on the Delaware devoted exclusively to the historical events that transpired there. I doubt there is another river in the United States more historic, while being singularly beautiful.

One should not neglect to mention as part of the river's history and importance that Philadelphia, located on the Delaware, was once the nation's capital and was where America's two most important documents were penned: the Declaration of Independence and the Constitution. Worth mentioning also is that the Hessian Barracks from the Revolutionary War is close by the river in Trenton. There was also the critical October 22, 1777, Battle of Red Bank on the river and river's edge in Gloucester Country and its importance in determining which army would control Philadelphia during the Revolutionary War. History is also represented by the presence of the World War II Battleship *New Jersey* berthed in Camden Harbor.

Besides history, there are unusual natural features along the Delaware. For example, just north of Milford, on River Road (Route 627) cacti grow on the red shale cliffs, and it is startling when one comes upon them growing out of the rock. They are the eastern prickly pear, sometimes called devil's tongue cacti, which in summer have brilliant yellow flowers and, by late fall, purple pear-shaped fruits. One wonders how these cacti tolerate the New Jersey winter. They are aided by the fact that a portion of River Road, known locally as The Narrows, is crowded by the 200-foot-high Milford Bluffs, which essentially make the road one-way for a brief period. A microclimate is created, especially because the area faces due South. While eastern prickly pear grows elsewhere in the East, they are the only cacti found this side of the Rocky Mountains.

Near the cacti are ancient, abandoned kilns built into the mountainside from which lime, the principal ingredient in cement, was extracted from limestone hundreds of years ago. The kilns and the cacti are the kinds of interesting things one regularly comes upon while tracing the Delaware's route. Along the river one may explore and find curious things forever.

The river's unusual features, history, and beauty are enhanced by its purity, one reason why America's Great Waters Coalition lists it as one of the nation's "great waters" on its list of only nineteen rivers and lakes. Also, in 2020, the American Rivers organization named the Delaware River of the Year. And the competition is stiff. There are approximately 3 million miles of rivers in the United States.

Lined by industry, especially along its more southern reaches, the river was not always clean and unpolluted. This area, including Trenton, Camden, Philadelphia, and Wilmington, was, from the late eighteenth to the early twentieth centuries, the industrial center of the United States. By the mid-twentieth century, the river was essentially bereft of life and infamous for its smell, which was so bad it was said to be discernible from low-flying small aircraft.

Flowering cacti growing in the rocks near the Delaware River.

Limestone Kilns, centuries old, carved into the wall of rocks near the river.

There are still large cities and industry along the river, but their emissions, now regularly policed, are remarkably clean. The river is no longer a conduit for garbage, human waste, and industrial runoff. Now fish are returning to the Delaware, and bald eagles in increasing numbers make their homes on its islands and forested banks. One will encounter other wildlife now flourishing along the river: hawks, beavers, otters, deer, black bears, and red foxes to name a few. In celebrating it, American Rivers wrote that, in its revived purity, "The Delaware River is a national success story." The Delaware's singular purity is especially to be celebrated when one considers the filthiness of such other New Jersey rivers as the Passaic, and, even more so, the recent declaration that the lower Hackensack River is a Superfund site.

One must salute the multitude of organizations dedicated to the river, especially the Delaware Riverkeeper Network, which passionately devotes itself to the health and beauty of the river and all its tributaries. For this organization, nature is not only to be preserved for human health and pleasure but itself has inherent rights. Other organizations concern themselves with the entire river, sections of it, or only a particular tributary, ranging from brooks to sizeable rivers that pour into the Delaware, amplifying its size. Among the latter, one thinks especially of the Lehigh, entering in Easton, Pennsylvania, the Schuylkill, entering in Philadelphia, and the Maurice (pronounced "Morris") entering in southern New Jersey.

Flowing south, the Delaware becomes wider and deeper. Luckily, the four states that border the river—New Jersey, New York, Pennsylvania, and Delaware—work together in the Delaware River Basin Commission headquartered in Trenton, New Jersey. The name of the organization teaches us something: that every drop of water that flows into a river is important, that the water of tributaries, from brooks to rivers, has much to do with determining the water quality of a major river such as the Delaware. The word "basin" suggests that the organization concerns itself with drainage in all of the 15,539 square miles of terrain in towns, counties, and states, every drop that might eventually make its way into the Delaware River. Poisonous substances emanating from any source, however small, can quickly ruin a river, if only temporarily. In late March 2023, Philadelphia residents were urged to only drink and cook using bottled water because of an 8,100-gallon spill of a toxic chemical into Otter Creek, a Delaware tributary north of the city.

Also, as we now know, grass fertilizer is a problem where it has runoff, which is almost everywhere it is utilized. This goes for insecticides even more so. We now know that these products have radically reduced the population of birds and butterflies, whose food is replaced by non-native plants they do not eat, has been made poisonous, or the insects they eat are greatly reduced or simply gone. A day may come when chemically treated lawns surrounding houses and other buildings are a thing of the past. Species are being eliminated around the globe. As we now know, given climate change, we may well be on the list in the not-too-distant future.

Enhancing both the Delaware's beauty and cleanliness is that it flows unhindered—without dams or obstructions—for all of its 331 miles, the longest free-flowing river east of the Mississippi, longer in this respect than the Hudson, longer than the Susquehanna. The Delaware, in the wake of the successful defeat of the proposal to build a dam at Tocks Island (chapter 5), was declared a Wild and Scenic River, a title shared by only a tiny percentage of our nation's rivers. The designation recognizes a river both as one of America's most beautiful and as particularly lending itself to adventure. Having canoed much of the river, including from its upper reaches to Philadelphia, participated twice in marathon-length races of homemade rafts, and regularly enjoyed the special sensation of swimming off some of its tiny beaches, gently carried along by the current, I can personally attest to this aspect of the river. I should also mention the lovely hiking trails following the river, making its surroundings an important part of its beauty. Walking a mile or two on a sandy Atlantic beach has its appeal but lacks the adventurous element of the beautiful forests along the Delaware, with their giant trees and boulders and wildlife (including birds of all the colors of the rainbow), waterfalls descending to the river, and mountains.

Besides its adventurous element, is there anything more relaxing and carefree than sitting in an inner tube and floating down a river, something provided at many upper river sites to individuals, families, and groups? And the Delaware is never crowded. I never feel freer than when I'm on the Delaware. Nor happier with the state of the world. The Delaware has always freely flowed, it flows thus today, and it will hopefully freely flow forever. In a chaotic world, there is comfort in that. Poets and philosophers celebrate naturally flowing rivers as the very embodiment of freedom and happiness.

Is there a child—or an adult—who has never thrown a stick into a river and, after following it and silently cheering it on for a distance, not found pleasure in imagining its future path and wished to be there to greet its arrival? Throwing a stick into a river is a simple but lovely substitute for setting sail on the river oneself. Of all the different bodies of water, I like rivers best because they're going somewhere, and I want to go where they're going.

The Delaware is fascinating to me from many points of view, and I hope readers who are unfamiliar with it will find it so as well. I have nothing against beaches. And it is fortunate, if not poetic, to have the sand and ocean on one side of the state and the woodlands, mountains, and a particularly beautiful river on the other. But I hope this book will awaken interest in and affection for the Delaware among those who do not know it well or at all. It provides further proof that the state is so much more than a broad strip of concrete stretching between New York, Philadelphia, and beyond, as out-of-staters, cruising the enormity of the New Jersey Turnpike, too often surmise.[1]

To entirely do the Delaware justice would take an encyclopedia. I'm going to discuss those aspects of the river and its Jersey culture that enthrall me, that I find most interesting. I hope I don't leave out something in those many extraordinary miles that some of you would have liked me to discuss. If so, you have my apologies and my hopes that you will, on your own, add to our knowledge of this wonderful river.

2

The Delaware
and New Jersey
Geography

In discussing the geography that the Delaware River is part of and informs, there are three matters that should first be addressed: how and when the river was discovered by Europeans and received the name by which it has been known ever since (including how New Jersey itself got its name); the Delaware's role in determining whether New Jersey is a peninsula; and the fact that, in effect, the river may be seen as divided into three different but continuous bodies of water.

The story of the river's name begins with Henry Hudson's visit to America in 1609. Representing the Dutch, Hudson, an Englishman, sailed to the entrance of Delaware Bay, where he weighed anchor for one night. Erroneously concluding the bay led to nothing of consequence, he turned his attention to the river that would one day bear his name. Dutch immigrants (the earliest Europeans to settle in New Jersey, quickly followed by the Swedes) were interested in both rivers, referring to the Delaware as the South River and the Hudson as the North River.

Henry Hudson's brief stop at the entrance to the Delaware was followed by that of Samuel Argall, an English sea captain who was more intrigued by it. In 1610 Argall sailed across the bay and part way up the river's estuary. Though the river had been called the Minisink by Native Americans, Argall named the river after the Royal Governor of the Virginia Colony, a nobleman, Thomas West, whose title was Baron De la Warr. For some years afterwards the English would largely refer to the river as the De la Warr, and that name slowly evolved into Delaware. In 1664, when the Dutch ceded their New Netherlands colony—headquartered on the southern tip of Manhattan Island and including much of New Jersey—to superior English forces, the river officially assumed the name it has had ever since. The State of Delaware also derived its name from the river, as did references by Europeans to the Lenape Indians who lived along much of it and were often referred to as "the Delawares."

If it is now understood why the river is called the Delaware, one might also ask where New Jersey got its name. The lands that would eventually be New Jersey were granted by the British crown to Sir George Carteret, who had until recently served as governor of the Isle of Jersey out in the English Channel and where Charles II, as his guest, hid from Cromwell. It was natural, then, for Carteret to name the colony, later to be a state, *New* Jersey. But there was a complication: Dutch and Swedish settlers were here before Carteret and his people. In 2014, New Jersey celebrated its 350th anniversary. But what it was really celebrating was the anniversary of when the British took it over from the Dutch. It is true that 1664 marks the beginning of when New Jersey was called New Jersey. But is there not a certain Anglo-Saxon bias in ignoring the original European settlers in New Jersey, the Dutch—not to mention the native peoples who preceded them by thousands of years?

As to the question of a peninsula, some of my fellow citizens consider New Jersey to be one, and the state is sometimes referred to in the media as such. It is, after all, relatively long and narrow and surrounded by water. A book on New Jersey's bridges calls New Jersey "a peninsula state, bordered east and west by the Hudson and Delaware Rivers."[1]

But New Jersey is not a peninsula. First, it is not attached to the continent by an isthmus, but by a wide part of the state, cutting across several counties. Also, a peninsula must be surrounded by continuous water of the same kind. New Jersey has the saltwater ocean on its eastern side and the largely freshwater Delaware River on its western. Though this is off topic, the reader might also be interested to learn that Cape May, named for Dutch explorer Cornelius Mey, often referred to as a peninsula, is also not one, for the same reasons the state is not. It is attached to the rest of New Jersey at its widest point, and while to one side of it is ocean, the other side is bordered by the mixed waters of Delaware Bay. But the waters of Delaware Bay at this point are almost identical to those of the ocean, so if the cape were attached by something narrow, I'd be willing to grant it peninsula status. But it isn't.

Real peninsulas are fairly rare. Sandy Hook is usually referred to as a peninsula, and we might as well call it one—though questions as to its legitimacy are raised by the Shrewsbury River, which once flowed entirely between it and the New Jersey mainland, so Sandy Hook, some geographers will argue, was earlier an island. However, a nineteenth-century shipwreck, and the sand and debris that accumulated around it, effectively closed off the Shrewsbury's access to the sea and, in effect, made Sandy Hook a peninsula. Whether it will always be one, or fierce stormwaters will someday reopen the river's access to the sea, turning the peninsula back into an island, remains a question to ponder.

Despite what I have said here, I regularly find people, even those with considerable geographic sophistication, referring to most of the land masses I've mentioned as peninsulas. I sympathize with them because I was one of them until I looked into the two key characteristics peninsulas must have: be connected to the mainland by an isthmus and surrounded by the same water on three sides. For them, and until now for me, if it looked like a peninsula, it was a peninsula. I'm genuinely sorry if this limited definition of a peninsula disturbs readers. Please feel free to think of certain landforms as peninsulas if you wish. A better idea might be the following: to call such places "peninsula-like," while maintaining the stricter (and geographically correct) definition of a peninsula.

As for the Delaware's three distinct personas: from its New York State origins to Trenton, it is 198 miles of freshwater, 121 miles of which border New Jersey. This is the most beautiful and exciting portion of the river. At Trenton it becomes an ever-broadening estuary, meaning that its freshwater from this point on is mixed with salt water. Tides coming in from the sea, on reaching that city, abruptly encounter eight-foot-high rapids that serve as a wall against further advance. They are often referred to as the Trenton Falls, but they are not a waterfall. As the ocean rises in response to climate change, it is possible that tidal surges reaching Trenton may someday pass over this obstacle, making the estuary extend to the north.

After passing Philadelphia and Wilmington plus considerably more miles, the river veers off to the east, broadening into a sizeable bay, mostly under New Jersey's Cumberland County. One might characterize the three portions of the Delaware lining New Jersey by the predominance of differing river traffic. In its northern portion, canoes and kayaks and rubber rafts are typical. In its middle portion are a preponderance of powerboats of all kinds, though in the nineteenth and early twentieth centuries many steamboats coursed through the waters of this middle section, especially carrying people and cargo between Philadelphia and Trenton. In the southern portion of the estuary and in the bay, one typically finds oceangoing traffic—tankers, cargo ships, etc.—entering and departing through the fourteen-mile opening between Cape May, New Jersey, and Cape Henlopen, Delaware, the initial pathway to the great industries of such towns as Wilmington and Philadelphia.

This last part of the Delaware creates a bit of a conflict in reckoning distances over the waters. I consider mile zero of the river to be at Hancock, New York, for that is where the west and east branches come together and, for me, the river begins. But seagoing vessels consider mile zero to be the entrance from the ocean into Delaware Bay. The Delaware River Basin Authority, representing the four states through which the Delaware flows (as well as the river's tributaries and their surrounds in that 15,539-square-mile area), considers the river as originating at the entrance to the bay from the sea. This is especially strange to any of us kayaking, canoeing, rafting, tubing, swimming, or fishing at any point from the river's northern origins as far south as Trenton. For us, rivers run downstream not up, and distances are calculated from their origins. But it is understandable why mariners might calculate distance from where they enter the Delaware—that is, from the mouth of its bay. Vessels of size will likely never travel the Delaware above Trenton, so it makes sense for them to begin calculating distances along the waters they traverse.

I should point out another anomaly. This book is titled *The Other Jersey Shore*, and its not-so secret agenda is to lure beachgoers away from their unqualified obsession with only one of New Jersey's two shores. But curiously, just as the Atlantic beaches of New Jersey conclude at Cape May, the Delaware, now in its large bay, ends on Cape May's western shore. Also, most of its land along Delaware Bay is sand and marsh and sports quite a number of largely unpopulated beaches. This means that, in effect, New Jersey's two shores, both ending at Cape May, might be seen as only one, ringing virtually all of New Jersey. I do not choose to see them this way, especially because one shore cannot be made up of two different waters, one mostly fresh and the other salt. The Delaware flows for most of its distance far from the Atlantic, and it is the Delaware River that intrigues me. But I felt a responsibility to remark on the irony of this strange circumstance, which all but challenges the title and purpose of this book.

While the book focuses on the West Jersey shore, the Delaware also courses through or borders three other states—New York, Pennsylvania, and Delaware. It begins in the Catskill Mountains, its West Branch passing through Pennsylvania, and then flows 77 miles till it reaches New Jersey, which it will border for the balance of its 331 miles.

The 77 miles before the river reaches New Jersey were not always certain, because where northwest New Jersey begins was debatable. New Jersey had argued with New York over this border since colonial times. Indeed, in the eighteenth century there were a series of skirmishes over the northern New Jersey border called the New York-New Jersey Line War. There was agreement from the start on the eastern border, a spot on the Palisades. To visit it you can park at the last Palisades Parkway rest area in New Jersey and hike north about a mile along a path close to the cliff, until you come across a stone monument in a wooded area. But New York, which has often acted in a superior, if not arrogant, manner toward New Jersey, its "country cousin," radically fancied the border to dip south from this point all the way down to today's Salem County, eliminating half of New Jersey. New Jersey more fairly insisted on a point slightly to the north along the Delaware where New York's Sullivan County town of Callicoon is located.

It was not until 1882 that the two states reached a compromise on New Jersey's northwestern border, based on a point at the southern tip of New York's town of Port Jervis at the edge of the Laurel Grove Cemetery and where the Neversink River enters the Delaware. Actually, New Jersey did not fare too badly in this agreement; its northern border is not straight across, east to west from the point on the Palisades, but angles slightly northward. In any case, there, on the Delaware's bank, virtually under Interstate 84, is the Witness Monument, an 1882 stone tablet tribute to the gentlemen who came to an agreement on this spot. A few feet away a rectangular granite stone, some eighteen inches long, also from 1882, officially marks the state line and points to another line: that between the two states on the one hand and Pennsylvania on the other.

The stone is referred to as the Tri-State Rock, but its tri-state function is not easily discernible. The border of New York and New Jersey with Pennsylvania is out in the middle of the river, hundreds of feet away. Thus, those who consider this monument as somewhat suggestive of Four Corners in the American Southwest, where Arizona, New Mexico, Utah, and Colorado converge, are a bit too sanguine. At Four Corners one may, in a prone position, actually place one's hands and feet in four states simultaneously. The only way to be in New York, New Jersey, and Pennsylvania simultaneously would be to kayak or swim out to the middle of the Delaware just opposite the tri-state monument. Of course, it would be near impossible, with any assurance, to locate that unmarked spot, and even if one could, extremely difficult to maintain one's position there given the river's current. One might almost wish the three states would mark the spot with a structure of some sort anchored to the bottom of the river, where a boater might temporarily tie on, or a swimmer grab hold. I don't anticipate this happening anytime soon. Hopefully, I have not spoiled the pleasure of those who locate the border stone and customarily stand on it believing they are in three states simultaneously. Sorry, not quite.

New Jersey and New York had long fought over their borders, not just at the Delaware. For example, New York insisted, until the U.S. Supreme Court told it otherwise in 1834, that its Hudson River border was the high-water mark on the Jersey shore, not the middle of the river—which, continuing down the coast, would have meant half of New Jersey's beaches were in New York. This is ironic today, when virtually all of the currently named Port of New York and New Jersey is in Newark and Elizabeth, New Jersey.[2]

New Jersey's perpetual struggles with New York over borders is not echoed by similar difficulties with Pennsylvania. The division between the two states, as already suggested, is simply the middle of the Delaware River.

Not so the State of Delaware. The division between New Jersey and Delaware is mostly the middle of the river, but there is a twelve-mile stretch where the river is wholly Delaware's. More surprising, there is a small chunk of the State of Delaware located in New Jersey.

How did this happen? In 1682, William Penn was intent on creating a definitive border between Pennsylvania and Delaware, having been granted land in both colonies by the crown. King Charles II agreed that a 12-mile circle emanating from the cupola of the courthouse in New Castle, Delaware, would be a fair delineation. Indeed, if one looks at where those states butt against each other today, the border is a perfect curving line, part of Penn's circle. But the circle continues across the Delaware River to the New Jersey shore. And not only here: the circle is completed twelve miles south of Delaware's border with Pennsylvania as well. So, while the river north

Young woman on the Tri-State Rock, just below Interstate 84.

and south of this line is divided down the middle, in this 12-mile section it is solely Delaware's. This means, in theory anyway, that if a fisherman around Pennsville, the nearest New Jersey town of any size, were to fish in these waters, he would technically need a Delaware license.

Things got particularly complicated when the Army Corps of Engineers, dredging the river in this area in the mid-twentieth century, dumped the silt on the limits of the Jersey shore. In effect, they created a now grassy outpost of the State of Delaware attached to New Jersey, about one-and-a-half miles long and a half-mile wide, known locally as The Point.

For years, neither state paid much attention to this anomaly. Then, in 1987, a hunter died inside this piece of land, ten feet from the New Jersey border. New Jersey police refused to deal with the matter, insisting that Delaware police come across the broad estuary of the river to recover the body which, they correctly insisted was Delaware's concern. Since then, when occasionally someone suicides off the Delaware Memorial Bridge, given the water currents, the body seems to unfailingly drift to this same area, and the Delaware police must retrieve the body. In addition, since this tiny piece of land is not patrolled, it has become a place where drugs are freely traded, alcohol drinking by New Jersey teenagers abounds, hunting occurs without regard to licensing or season, and people in the area have had the habit of abandoning nonfunctioning automobiles and other junk there.

The Army Corps of Engineers was prevailed upon to put up what has proven to be an entirely porous fence and to dig a shallow ditch around the area, which is inadequate for keeping out anyone who wishes to enter from the New Jersey side. No one has bothered to put up signs saying WELCOME TO DELAWARE or WELCOME TO NEW JERSEY for people entering or exiting this tiny piece of land, so New Jerseyans who wander into it have no idea that they are in Delaware.

Neither state really wants or needs this piece of land, but both stubbornly believe there is a principle to be observed. So much so, that the issue has been before the U.S. Supreme Court three times. In each case the court affirmed the 1682 Penn scheme: this little piece of added land, attached to New Jersey, was indeed Delaware's, with only Samuel Alito and the late Antonin Scalia arguing that the land was part of New Jersey and that it would be convenient for both states to make it so. Probably true, but Alito's and Scalia's dissenting votes, given that they were both native New Jerseyans, are proof, as often alleged, that the Supreme Court often makes decisions based on personal views or common sense rather than legal precedent or the

Constitution. The most recent case concerning this errant piece of land was in 2005, and the Supreme Court signaled in its judgement that this was it; it was no longer willing to hear testimony on this all but inconsequential matter,

But a running joke continues between the two states. New Jersey pretends that Delaware must have invaded it at some point in its history, Delaware arguing that New Jersey must not with its greater size and population be allowed to overpower Delaware's sovereignty. The Delaware State Legislature has demanded, tongue in cheek, that the National Guard be called out to protect this piece of land against New Jersey "usurpers." New Jersey has responded that if this is done the World War II Battleship *New Jersey*, anchored in Camden Harbor, will be sent down the river to settle the matter. The situation is further complicated by the fact that the Army Corps of Engineers may well add to the disputed land from time to time by further dredging of the river in the twelve-mile area where the waters, and what is beneath them, are wholly Delaware's and it is again convenient to dump the river bottom's contents on the New Jersey side. So, Delaware's presence in New Jersey may grow over time and that chunk of land may be a source of contention between the two states for centuries to come. One can imagine this as a worthy theme for a comic opera.

Both states must breathe a metaphoric sign of relief when those twelve miles of the river end, and the river and subsequent bay are once again neatly divided down the middle and there is no further source of conflict. One wonders whether the peace-loving Quaker William Penn had the slightest notion that establishing Pennsylvania's border with Delaware in the fashion chosen was going to cause trouble, even of the lightest kind, between Delaware and New Jersey for more than 300 years.

Islands in the Stream

I am aware that in choosing the title for this chapter I am pirating both the title of a posthumously published Ernest Hemingway novel and a country music song Dolly Parton recorded with Kenny Rogers, but it did seem appropriate to what the chapter is about: the islands that populate the Delaware River, with a focus on those in New Jersey waters.

As best I can determine, there are presently 194 islands, counting even the tiny inconsequential ones. I say "presently" because islands in a rapidly flowing river are forever emerging and growing or declining and disappearing—especially the latter when they are not long established and have no trees, bushes, or other greenery whose roots hold them together. Flooding may destroy an island almost as it does a house on the banks of the river. Drought or steady silting also affects the number and character of islands.

Only 87 of the 194 islands are named according to the Delaware River Basin Commission; there are others that were once named but today belong only to history. For example, George Washington hid the Durham boats he used for his several Delaware crossings behind Malta Island, just off the Pennsylvania shore. The British Army could not see them from the New Jersey shore and prepare for potential attacks. The island no longer exists, the space between it and the shore having slowly silted in. Too bad; it might have warranted a small monument.

Three islands have special significance to me, and I will focus on them in this chapter. Two are in New Jersey waters, and the third would be in New Jersey waters except for its location within that William Penn–inspired border circle discussed in the previous chapter, which technically places it in the State of Delaware. The two New Jersey islands are Lewis Island, at the edge of the town of Lambertville, where a shad fishery functions in season on a daily basis; and Burlington Island, believed to be the very first place of European settlement in New Jersey (the Dutch). Fort Delaware Island, also known as Pea Patch Island, is the one technically in Delaware waters although it is closer to New Jersey. Though Fort Delaware, with its massive fort, was never involved in battle, it became the main Union Army site for Confederate prisoners of war, most of whom were captured at Gettysburg.

The Lewis Fishery Island

This is a small, narrow island whose southern end is a hundred yards or so north of the New Hope-Lambertville Bridge. The island is formally named Holcombe Island, because it was originally owned by a certain Richard Holcombe who initiated fishing there back in 1771. William Lewis Sr. began fishing with the Holcombes, and, by 1888, he had taken over the fishery and by 1918 had purchased the southern half of the island. From that point on no Holcombes seem to have interested themselves in the island or the fishery or even appeared there. Today, few people call it anything but Lewis Island.

To make things complicated, Lewis Island is not always an island. Between it, the Delaware and Raritan Canal feeder, and the town is a narrow waterway called simply Island Creek. When it is running strong—sometimes complemented by another creek or by waters from the Delaware River—the circle of the island is complete, but when there's a drought or low water, the circle may be incomplete, and then the island is, in effect, a peninsula. But no one pays attention to this. Lewis Island is Lewis Island, regardless of current circumstances.

When Bill Lewis, the great-grandfather of the present captain of the crew, established the fishery, he obtained a still valid 1888 license from the State of New Jersey. Today, it is the only legal shad net fishery north of Trenton tidewater. William's son Fred next took over the fishery. Fred's daughter Muriel followed, and she is presently the owner of the Lewis family's portion of the island. Her husband, David Meserve, died before his father-in-law did, so he never became captain. Now David and Muriel's son, Steve Meserve, is captain of the fishery. The fifth generation (kids, really) is too young to provide leadership but actively participates in the fishing with pride in their heritage.

The family has two structures on the island, a house where Lewis family or friends have occasionally lived and a fishing shack where nets, hip boots, and other equipment are stored and from which shad is sold when there has been a large haul. During the summer, when there is no shad fishing (the shad have migrated north), the shack is found at the center of what is known as Lewis Island beach, which is crowded with swimmers, the shack selling refreshments that help keep the fishery going. Steve Meserve and his crew fish every day in season, which is mostly in the spring, when the shad are swimming upriver to spawn.

Fishing is constrained by bad weather and the condition of the river. Wind can sometimes make the river too rough or, after a heavy rain or hurricane, too deep. But if fishing was not done regularly, the family would lose its venerable license. That is unlikely to happen. Steve and the others fish because they love it and because they cherish their participation in a family tradition.

It is the dedicated activities of the Lewis family over four generations and 135 years that has brought extra attention to the island. Indeed, the fishery inspired a book by a Lambertville resident, Charlie Groth, a folklorist who teaches across the river at Bucks County Community College. Her book focuses on the cultural and community significance of the fishery, which attracts a good number of volunteers, happy to be involved in any way they can be helpful.[1] In the course of writing her book, Groth became a regular member of the fishing crew and today is one of those who helps haul in the net after it has been spread and maneuvered over the water. She also takes on other tasks as needed, the enthusiasm of her work emblematic of the charm of her book.

Rod and reel fishermen up and down the river also go after shad, the largest fish in the herring family. Landing a hooked fish is a challenge. Indeed, the *New Yorker* writer John McPhee wrote a book on his shad fishing adventures on the Delaware (or perhaps his misadventures) titled *The Founding Fish*, in which he quotes an old saying about shad, that it is "pound for pound, the fightn'st fish around." He talks at one point about some folks who walked across the New Hope-Lambertville Bridge when he was trying to land a fighting shad just below. After significant time in New Hope, they discovered on their return that he was still at it with the same fish.[2]

Female fish are greater fighters than males, and larger—adults range between three to eight pounds, while male adults range from three to five pounds. Females are also known as roe fish because their eggs are prized as a gastronomic delicacy. Once hooked, like marlin or other deep-sea fish, shad will often leap high above the water, attempting to free themselves or turn sideways in hopes the river current will free them. Considerable time may pass before they may be brought aboard one's boat. McPhee talks about how it often took him an hour.

Shad are ocean fish who migrate up the Delaware to spawn in freshwater in April and May, some traveling all the way north to the very origins of the river. As they migrate, rod and reel fishermen are waiting for them, and so are the folks on Lewis Island. In the early fall the adult fish descend the river and head out to sea, so there is a second, more limited fishing season, usually in October. If the little ones, recently hatched, are caught in the net, they are immediately returned to the river.

During and in the years following World War II the lower Delaware was so polluted by human and industrial waste from Trenton, Philadelphia, and Wilmington that shad could not get past the oxygen-starved waters to spawn upriver, and it appeared as if they had died off. In recent years, however, since the river became one of the cleanest in America, the shad have been coming back.

I had the good fortune of being invited to Lewis Island by Charlie Groth in the spring of 2021. To get there I crossed a bridge over the Delaware and Raritan Canal feeder at Coryell Street, and then the smaller, wooden one across Island Creek and onto the island. The wooden one is sometimes wiped out or seriously damaged by high water accompanying hurricanes or nonstop rainstorms. It is quickly repaired or replaced by the fishing crew. The narrow southern tip of the island is roughly paved for some twenty-five feet to ensure firm footing and to preclude sinking in the mud, important after a heavy rainstorm and critical when the island is recovering from a flood. If the river is high enough it will cover much of the island and this paved strip as well.

Except for weekends, the Lewis crew fish in the late afternoon or early evening. Finishing their regular jobs for the day, they head for the island. As Steve Meserve puts it, "I work in a cubicle all day"—for most of his career

Steve was a computer programmer; he is currently a business analyst—"so I can't wait to get out in nature and just enjoy the river and the fishing. I always say to crew members, 'Another day in paradise,' regardless of what luck we've had. I also love being part of this family tradition and will do it as long as I can. Then I'll turn it over to the next generation. Given our expenses, we don't make any money on the fishery. I guess you could say this is our hobby—but it's more than that. Being part of a tradition gives meaning to your life."

Steve's pride in the fishery is indicated by his putting out an e-mail report on each day's haul, which I receive and read with pleasure. The fishery seems like a remnant of an earlier America in which community feeling was more present, when people gathered to raise barns and neighbors weren't just people who happened to live next door. Lewis Island is as much a community as a fishery.

It was quite an inspiring sight watching the Lewis crew work. A rowboat, with two women aboard keeping it going straight, is towed upriver against the current some hundred yards by a thick rope held by several men hugging the shore. The top rope at the end of the net is passed to a strong man on shore who is aided by wearing a leather harness. At this point, two or three men replace the women in the boat, one or two rowing and the other, usually Steve Meserve, in the back with the carefully coiled net. Now the rowboat, fighting the current, heads straight across the river. The net has floats on top and lead weights on the bottom so that, under ideal conditions, it stands vertically in the river. The maximum depth of the river for fishing is 4.4 feet. Above that level, usually after heavy rainstorms, the river is moving too fast to guarantee safe conditions and it is likely that sticks or even a large object, such as a log, will become entangled in the net, which may ruin the net or at least require substantial work to remove the log, likely spoiling the fishing for that day. The river is almost never too low to fish following the customary channel off Lewis Island. If it's too high, fishing will likely be called off for that day because the shad will be passing under the net.

The net is cast out by Meserve, the man on shore laboring against the current to keep the net straight. Ideally, the bottom of the net hugs the bottom of the river, the floats keeping its top just at the surface. Halfway across the river the rowboat turns south while the man on shore, holding the rope and keeping the net as taut as he can, also retreats downriver. When he gets to the south end he hands his rope to the crew that will haul in the net, which is now in the shape of the letter C. The rowboat heads into shore, its

Steve Meserve and his Lewis Island crew. Steve is at the back of the boat carefully casting out the net.

crew hoping shad are trapped in the net. They turn over their end of the net, making a U-shape. The shore crew, now joined by the men who were in the boat, begin hauling in the net. Now the net is reduced to the shape of a large bag, and thrashing about in it are the shad. As soon as the shad are cleared from the net, crew members inspect the net, removing any foreign objects such as twigs, rocks, or larger debris. They may soon begin sewing together any parts that may have gotten torn and then lay out the net to dry.

As for the shad that were caught, some are distributed among the crew, though when there is an excess it is sold and the crew may each receive some pocket change. No one participates to get fish or money but simply to be part of the occasion. The fishery is like a club, with Captain Steve Meserve its current president.

Fishing for migrating shad in the Delaware has a long history, going back hundreds, if not thousands, of years. The Lenape fished for shad with nets weighted by stones with nicks in them instead of lead weights. George Washington was an avid shad fisherman on a semiprofessional basis as a young man. His familiarity with the fish and how to catch them would come in handy later when he needed to feed his starving army as it camped along the Delaware. Close to when the Lewis family secured its license, Thomas

Members of the volunteer crew pulling in a haul with both ends of the net in close. Watching the action are neighbors, friends, and visitors attending the annual Lambertville Shad Fest.

Eakins, headquartered at the Pennsylvania Academy for the Fine Arts in Philadelphia, crossed the Delaware in 1881, setting up his easel on the riverbank to paint fishermen in hip waders deploying nets, much as Native Americans once did, to catch shad.

The two sides of the river enjoyed a close relationship then, as they do today. This was especially true downriver between Philadelphia and Camden. There were no bridges, but the river was full of boats, including regular ferries between the two cities. Every day, Eakins crossed the Delaware from Philadelphia on a ferry to paint his classic portrait of Walt Whitman (1887–1888) at his home in Camden, New Jersey, close by the Delaware. America's great poet lived in Camden during his final years, and his tomb is there.

Burlington Island

Burlington Island, midriver and just off the town of Burlington, is the second-largest Delaware River island, 1.2 kilometers long and totaling 408 acres when the large, manmade lake at its center is included. Statistics about the island vary, with some using the figure 311 acres, not counting the lake as part of the island's dimensions.

The island was once an active resort. It reached its peak in the 1920s, with a host of cabins, a beach, and a large amusement park featuring a roller coaster and a Ferris wheel. A children's summer camp was established. There was even a miniature railway. Thousands of people, mostly from Trenton and Philadelphia, visited it in summer, arriving in steamboats that docked at the island. Both arrival and departure had to happen at high tide.

But a series of fires in 1928 and 1934 destroyed the island's main attractions, leaving it covered with mountains of debris. One of the key items that was saved was the beautiful merry- go-round, which was moved in 1932 to Seaside Heights on that other New Jersey shore. What remained were summer settlers on the island, some sixty primitive cabins shared by eighty-five families, and a few other structures. These remained until 1978 when the decision was made to return the island to wilderness. Had this not been done, there were developers waiting in the wings to develop the whole island at a great loss to its natural character.

Cabin residents had never owned the land on which their structures stood and they paid weekly rentals to the Board of Island Managers. Thus, those with cabins and other structures who were evicted, though disappointed, were not in a position to aggressively resist returning the island to its origins. But the massive cleanup of the remains of the amusement park continues. At a 2019 cleanup by volunteers, 97,000 pounds of junk, mostly twisted, rusted metal, were removed.

But as one walks around the island today it becomes obvious that much more awaits removal. There is ruin everywhere, including piles of rusted metal and foundations of homes and other buildings. There is even an abandoned radio station where former radio and television personality, as well as State Senator and 2021 candidate for Lieutenant Governor on the Republican ticket, Diane Lane, used to be ferried out for regular broadcasts, which kept Burlington Island in the public eye.

I was invited out to the island by Jim McCreary, who serves as president of the Board of Island Managers. We traveled in a pontoon boat, which had to time its landing and departure to the three hours before and after high tide. If one arrived or left at any other time there could be as much as forty feet of mud to cross before we could access the island or return to the boat.

In a sense, Jim's position has existed since 1682 when the Dutch, the first European settlers in New Jersey, organized their settlement on the island

With Jim McCreary steering, the pontoon boat moves out toward Burlington Island from Burlington town.

A typical pile of rusted metal left from the days when Burlington Island harbored a giant amusement park. With the help of volunteers, the island will, in the not-too-distant future, be cleared and returned to its original wilderness state.

into a community, preferring the island to the mainland for security reasons. Arriving at the dawn of the seventeenth century, the Dutch were in New Jersey well before the British. They briefly considered the island their headquarters in America—though Peter Minuit in effect overruled this decision with his purchase from Native Americans of the southern portion of Manhattan Island, creating New Amsterdam, with its outlying portions, such as those in New Jersey, called New Netherlands. In Manhattan, the Dutch built a stockade across the island for security from attacks on what we still call Wall Street.

The importance of the Dutch in New York and New Jersey has always been largely ignored, partly the result of an Anglo-Saxon bias in our history. The British took over New Jersey from the Dutch in 1664. The statewide celebration of 350 years of history in 2014 should really have been seen as simply a celebration of the naming of New Jersey. There is a reason there are so many Dutch Reformed churches scattered throughout New Jersey and that Rutgers, the state university, was originally simply a Dutch Reformed seminary. One still adjoins the university's main campus in New Brunswick.

Dutch hegemony of Burlington Island was first challenged when Swedes began to settle there, as they did throughout southern New Jersey. Let us not forget that New Jersey has to this day a town with the name Swedesboro. In any case, one could say that the town of Burlington, with some ten thousand residents today, began on the island.

But things are even more complicated. The city of Burlington was first called Burlington Island because it was surrounded by water, including inlets from the river and creeks that circled the town. So, in a sense, there once were two Burlington islands. What we now know as the island continued for years to bear its Lenape name of *Matinicunk*, which means "Island of the Pines." When the mainland creeks were placed underground, the town was no longer an island, certainly not visibly so. So, understanding just what was/is Burlington Island and Burlington town is a tricky and confusing business. Judith Gauntt, a historian and member of the Friends of Burlington Island, actually discovered a 1690 deed of two hundred acres of Burlington Island belonging to her ancestors, only to learn that it was not what is currently the island referred to but territory on the mainland in what is now the city of Burlington.

Early on, Quakers arrived in numbers and became a dominant group in Burlington town; they are still important in western New Jersey and, of course, across the river in Pennsylvania. They had a commitment to education and built a number of public schools that were likely the first ones in America. One doesn't want to minimize the contributions of Horace Mann to public education—first in Massachusetts and then spreading across the young nation—but the Quakers in Burlington were building public schools there many decades before Mann advocated for them.

When the city of Burlington was established, the island remained something of a separate entity. On the other hand, Burlington town has so much history of its own that it is understandable that, over time, residents would pay less attention to the island. Folks in Burlington are more likely to talk about the town being the birthplace of America's first novelist of importance, James Fenimore Cooper, as well as the birthplace of Captain James Lawrence, commander of the USS *Chesapeake* during the War of 1812. Mortally wounded, he was celebrated for his heroic last words, "Don't give up the ship!" Both their homes are preserved as part of the Burlington County Historical Society, which also has two other buildings.

Another home of historical significance was that of General, later President, Ulysses S. Grant. His family resided in Burlington during much of the Civil War to keep them away from the battlefields. Grant joined them occasionally. He and his wife had been invited to accompany Abraham Lincoln to Ford's Theatre on the fateful night of Lincoln's assassination but had respectfully declined so Grant could be with his children. En route to Burlington, Grant learned, in Philadelphia, of the tragic news and returned to the nation's capital. It is uncertain just when. One source has Grant immediately turning around. However, in Grant's own two volume memoirs he says he quickly took a train up to Burlington, spent an hour or so with his children, who he had not seen for months, and then he left his wife and children and took a train back to Philadelphia and another on to Washington. One wonders if, given his immense experience as a soldier, Grant would have been able to stop Lincoln's assassin, or at least made sure that the negligent bodyguard remained at his post outside the box for as long as Lincoln was there. Grant's Burlington house is still intact but in private hands.

Burlington is also the headquarters of the West Jersey Proprietors, descendants of the 1664 British settlers when New Jersey was divided into East and West Jersey by the crown. It was in effect two royal colonies, with Burlington the capital of West Jersey and Perth Amboy the capital of East Jersey. To this day, any land in what was West Jersey that is not privately or publicly owned, with the papers to prove it, is Proprietor territory, and every once in a while, if a piece of land is discovered that has no deed, it belongs to the Proprietors. They may sell it, and use the money to maintain their beautiful old building, where they keep their ancient records.

Burlington is a particularly interesting town but also an interesting county. It is New Jersey's largest and the only one that extends across the state from the Delaware River to the Atlantic Ocean.

Jim McCreary's position as president of the Board of Managers is one to which he is elected by the citizens of Burlington. His board is the oldest continuously operated land trust board anywhere in the United States. Only recently, in 1953, was ownership of the island transferred to the City of Burlington. Until then it was politically independent of the city. The town thenceforth has paid more attention to its celebrated island.

In addition to the Board of Managers, which has meetings in Burlington City twice a month, there are the Friends of Burlington Island, which lends its support. It supplies volunteers to continue the task of cleaning up the island and is eternally mindful of those who might try to use the island as a dumping ground. It is particularly concerned that the Army Corps of Engineers might use the island for its river dredgings—a problem which, as already suggested, is a universal one up and down the river, especially in the twelve-mile circle that, luckily, Burlington Island is not within.

Access to the island is today theoretically restricted to those approved by the Board of Managers—a situation that is likely to continue indefinitely or until the island is cleared of its debris and turned into a nature preserve. Nevertheless, people regularly land on it in canoes and kayaks, both from the New Jersey and Pennsylvania sides, especially from Burlington and the town of Bristol, Pennsylvania, which is just on the other side of the island, directly across the river from Burlington. A number of people living in Bristol are active in the Friends of Burlington Island. Some visitors, legally or not, come to camp out, others to hike its trails. There are four distinct trails one can explore for a total of five miles. For safety's sake, steel markers have been placed along these trails so that if someone is seriously injured they can tell rescuers exactly where they are.

The most curious thing about the island is its large and beautiful ninety-seven-acre lake, which will eventually be made freely available for recreation activities. Hiking the island, one wonders how it is that a large lake is in it, largely toward one end. The lake was created when particularly rich sand in this part of the island was excavated by construction companies and the large hole created was filled by natural springs and water seeping in from the Delaware River. Until recently, the lake had a small opening to the river, but this was judged to be unnecessary and allowed motorboats to come off the river into the lake, bringing noise and pollution with them and changing the character of the lake and the island itself. The opening to the river was closed off. Now the island, on maps or from the air, looks like a Dutch clog, the lake being where one would insert their foot.

The current plan is to return the island as much as possible to its original, natural state. Walking the trails of the island, I was never sure when I was staring at the lake or at the river itself. There is uncertainty among those who know the island well as to whether the creation of the lake gave the island a superb amenity or simply made it strange. Whichever it is, the lake gives the island a unique quality, and it's clear that it will someday be a superb site for swimming, without the swift current that makes swimming in the river more challenging.

What I felt on the island and in conversation with various officers and volunteers is the immense spirit of these folks, and the pleasure they get from their dedication. It is no accident that on the Board of Managers' website is an inspiring quote from President Obama: "Change will not come if we wait for some other person or some other time. We are the ones we've been waiting for. We are the change we seek." Amen to that.

Pea Patch Island, Fort Delaware, and Finn's Point Cemetery

The reason the island containing Fort Delaware is called Pea Patch Island is that, allegedly, a vessel got stuck on a marshy shoal attached to the island in the eighteenth century, and the only way the crew could set it afloat was to lighten it by dumping its cargo of peas. Soon the island was overrun with pea plants and, as these grew over the years, the island slowly became larger to the point where it is now 247 acres and a mile long and half a mile wide. Whether the pea patch story is true or a legend remains uncertain. I'd settle for a tall tale. As far as I can see, no peas grow on the island today.

For many years there was a struggle over ownership of the island. First a gentleman from New York produced papers showing that he had inherited it. When he eventually abandoned his claim out of an absence of interest, New Jersey and Delaware fought over the island, which is in the middle of the river, slightly closer to New Jersey. But, as already mentioned, the federal government declared it to be Delaware's because it falls just within the by now familiar Penn border circle of 1682.

Delaware, in turn, ceded the primary use of the island to the federal government to build its fort on the south end, but it continues to maintain the Pea Patch Island Nature Preserve on the island's north side, which includes one of the largest mixed species bird sanctuaries in the eastern United States, especially for wading birds such as ibises and egrets, with herons, bald eagles, and osprey as well. This is one of the attractions for tourists taking a ferry out to the island from Delaware City, Delaware, or Fort Mott, New Jersey, sometimes as part of a multi-fort expedition including a third fort, Delaware's Fort Dupont.

From its federal takeover, the main purpose of the island was military. Fort Delaware was the largest American army fort ever built up to that time. Located just before the two-mile-wide estuary enters Delaware Bay, the island's fort, loaded with heavy cannon, was perfectly positioned as a bulwark against attacks on Wilmington and Philadelphia. It was particularly important during the Civil War, but also during World War II, when it helped ward off German U-boats that preyed upon American shipping, especially that entering or departing Delaware Bay. It also blocked enemy submarines from proceeding across the bay and up the river. Had these submarines been able to do so, they could have attacked the chemical industries of Wilmington and the large and critically important military shipbuilding facilities in Philadelphia's harbor.

As it was, some eighteen American ships of all kinds were sunk during World War II just off Cape May or at the beginnings of the Atlantic just beyond Delaware Bay, with a loss of 6,000 American sailors. Some of the ships were sunk by mines the Germans distributed in the waters at the entrance to Delaware Bay. The presence of Nazi submarines up and down the Atlantic coast during World War II was something rarely discussed by the Pentagon or in the media, apparently to avoid panic. Most Americans did not know during the war that the Nazis were actually right off our coast.[3]

An advantage America had was the Chesapeake and Delaware Canal, connecting the two great bays. Built in 1829, it was serviceable during World War II and even today extends from Delaware Bay (not far from Pea Patch Island) over to Chesapeake City. It continues as part of the intracoastal waterway. It is just fourteen miles across that narrow neck of Delaware, saving a 300-mile trip around the Delmarva Peninsula if one needed to get from, say, Philadelphia or Wilmington to Baltimore. In World War II, in addition to saving much time and fuel, it saved lives and ships, transporting goods needed elsewhere by an inland route not exposed to German submarines. The canal effortlessly supported the defenses of Fort Delaware and vice versa.

Fort Delaware was built on Pea Patch Island in 1819 but burned down in 1831. The new fort, constructed between 1846 and 1848, was solidly built of stone and brick with a moat around it. Given the soft and marshy soil of the island, with parts of it actually lower than the island high tide line, wooden piles were hammered into the ground and a platform built on top of them to ensure that the fort, built atop the platform, would not slowly sink.[4]

During the early years of the Civil War, it became obvious the Confederacy did not have enough of a Navy to menace Wilmington and Philadelphia, so the fort largely gave up its strictly defense function and became a prison. A total of 12,500 Confederate prisoners were kept at the fort, though its facilities could only adequately handle 4,000. A few of its prisoners were not soldiers from the South but New Jersey Confederate sympathizers. Early in the war, prisoners were sensibly exchanged, a procedure later abandoned because the two sides could not agree on a continuing workable procedure and animosity grew as the war continued on.[5]

Although more than one historian argues that as many as 200–300 Confederate soldiers escaped from Fort Delaware, I believe this to be a gross exaggeration. At most, only several dozen prisoners escaped. One authoritative source puts the figure at fifty-six.[6] A good swimmer might be able to manage the one mile to the New Jersey shore, or a little farther to the Delaware shore, but the current increased the challenge. Some escapees surely drowned. Others may have crossed the frozen ice in winter, the water in the estuary and bay being sufficiently unsalted so as to occasionally freeze solid enough. Ironically, once ashore they were helped by an organization whose informal name was identical to the hallowed name we all know and celebrate under different circumstances: the Underground Railroad. This one was managed by Confederate sympathizers who were devoted to getting Fort Delaware escapees back to the South and, when possible, to their fighting units.[7]

One must remember that slavery was still practiced in New Jersey, especially in South Jersey but throughout the state, from its earliest days until the end of the Civil War and the ratification of the Thirteenth Amendment in early 1865—which the New Jersey legislature initially opposed. As a New Jerseyan I'm ashamed to admit that New Jersey was the last northern state to completely outlaw slavery.[8] Even after the Thirteenth Amendment to the United States Constitution was passed, it was not until January 23, 1866, that a new governor, Marcus L. Ward, signed an amendment to the New Jersey Constitution officially ending slavery in the state. However, in the state's defense, as early as 1804 the legislature passed the Gradual Abolition of Slavery Law, so that by the time Ward signed the amendment there were very few people still enslaved. The 1860 census lists sixteen enslaved people. New York City had outlawed slavery as early as 1827, so the enslaved in New Jersey often fled there.

But the persistence of slavery until that point may account, in part, for the shocking fact that in both the 1860 and 1864 elections, the state did not vote for Abraham Lincoln. In 1864 it voted for George McClellan, the former head of the Union Army who had proven such a disappointment to Lincoln in the early days of the war and whom Grant replaced. After the war McClellan became governor of New Jersey.

Today there is continuing discussion about differences between North and South Jersey, somewhat modified by the longtime assertion that there is also a Central New Jersey.[9] One can see that some of the differences between North and South Jersey may have been enhanced by the fact that slavery was more abundant and continued longer in South Jersey and that there were Confederate sympathizers there, especially in Salem County.

A total of 2,502 prisoners died at Fort Delaware, especially from cholera or smallpox, both exacerbated by the crowded conditions. Additionally, 135 Union Army guards sickened and died, most succumbing to these two diseases as well.

Fort Delaware has been likened in its treatment of prisoners to Andersonville, the notorious prisoner of war camp for Union soldiers, in Georgia. Dr. S. Weir Mitchell, the federal inspector of prisons, wrote to his sister: "Fort Delaware is to the South what Andersonville . . . is to the north, a cesspool of misery, dirt, lice, rats and disease. Tomorrow I go to Fort Delaware to inspect that inferno of detained rebels. All twelve thousand to an island that should hold four thousand . . . twenty deaths a day . . . and the living having more life on them than in them."[10]

Fort Delaware was certainly a horror, but that it was the equal of Andersonville may be something of an exaggeration. Of the 45,000 Union prisoners at Andersonville, some 13,000 died, a good number of starvation, with little or no provision of food, clothing, medical attention, and shelter, abetted by utterly gratuitous mistreatment that was often sadistic. Many Andersonville survivors were reduced to skin and bones and, when liberated, looked like the barely alive survivors of Nazi concentration camps, while Confederate prisoners at Fort Delaware were fed more decently, most dying of disease.

The 2,502 Confederate soldiers who died at Fort Delaware were close to one-fifth of the island's occupants, while at Andersonville closer to one-third of the prisoners died. The commander of the Andersonville prison was accused of war crimes and tried and hanged at the end of the Civil War. The commandant of Fort Delaware might have been executed as well had the South won the war or at least taken over the island, because he was also known for his senseless cruelty and was nicknamed General Terror by Confederate prisoners. So, Fort Delaware's treatment of prisoners was unacceptable, something Northerners, who solely condemn Andersonville in textbooks, are generally loathe to admit.

Of course, there were many more Union Army prisons for Confederate soldiers besides Fort Delaware and Confederate prisons for Union soldiers besides Andersonville. In total, some 56,000 Union and Confederate soldiers died during their wartime imprisonment, a shameful, inexcusable lack of humanity shown by both sides. Among the Union Army prisons was the star-shaped Fort Wood, built just before the War of 1812 on Bedloe's Island in the New York–New Jersey harbor. Imprisoned Confederate soldiers died there as well. The irony of this island's name later being changed to Liberty Island and housing the Statue of Liberty (mounted atop a now solid and filled in Fort Wood at its base) is almost too much to tolerate. One wonders how many, if any, of the millions of annual visitors to Liberty Island are aware of this dark chapter in the island's history.

The dead at Fort Delaware were at first buried on the island, but given its general marshiness, a more suitable small cemetery was opened in 1863 at Finn's Point on the New Jersey bank of the Delaware River. It is near the town of Pennsville in Salem County, surrounded by the Killcohook National Wildlife Refuge, an Army Corps of Engineers facility. Finn's Point got its name because there was once a small settlement of Finnish Americans there. This annex to Fort Delaware is six miles north of the town of Salem and adjoins Fort Mott (created during the Spanish-American War and since 1951 a state park). You reach the stone walled cemetery after passing through the main gates of the park.

The base of the eighty-five-foot-high Confederate monument at Finn's Point National Cemetery, with the names of the 2,436 Confederate soldiers who died in captivity on Pea Patch Island at Fort Delaware who are buried in mass graves in front of the monument. Looking closely at the far left one may just make out the marble tombstones of the Nazi soldiers and Russian adherents to the Nazi cause, several of whom hanged themselves and others who were shot in a riot. Jim Turk, who led me to this spot, is observing the monument.

A government tugboat, the *Osceola*, brought as many of the Fort Delaware dead as it could carry over to Finn's Point each day. A total of 2,436 Confederates were buried there, their remains interred in mass graves created from deep ditches. There is no sign of individual graves today, just a well-tended grass lawn that one cannot help but step on to cross the cemetery. However, the names of the dead Confederates are inscribed on bronze plaques on the concrete base of an eighty-five foot granite obelisk monument that was erected in 1910, making of the Finn's Point Cemetery something of a Confederate shrine.

While there is also a marble memorial erected in 1879 to the Union soldiers serving as guards who died at Fort Delaware, with their names inscribed on it, I must admit that, as a Yankee, I had strange feelings coming across what is largely a Confederate graveyard in New Jersey. Finn's Point is annually visited by the United Daughters of the Confederacy, who raised the money to pay for the bronze plaques with the names of the 2,436 Confederate dead on the base of the monument and routinely lay wreaths there. They are also allowed by federal law to put up a modest Confederate flag once a year on Memorial Day, as long as it is at a lesser height and size than the Stars and Stripes. Surprisingly, this privilege is allowed similar organizations at national cemeteries with Confederate dead around the country. Organizations must apply each year for permission. However, Memorial Day is celebrated at some of these cemeteries on different dates than that celebrated elsewhere in the country because of contrary Southern notions of what were the key dates in the Civil War period.

The United Daughters of the Confederacy, very much still in existence, and at least until recently alleged to be Ku Klux Klan supporters, is headquartered in Richmond, Virginia. They sponsor an auxiliary, the United Children of the Confederacy, which the Daughters describe as dedicated to teaching children about their "heritage," especially encouraging them to associate themselves with the Lost Cause idea. In 2020, the headquarters building was attacked and set afire during a Black Lives Matter demonstration against the murder of George Floyd by Minneapolis police.

I'm sure this happens elsewhere as well, but I learned that there are visitors to Finn's Point Cemetery who come when they wish and quickly insert multiple small Confederate flags into the ground, but these are taken down immediately by the cemetery caretaker.

Not only Civil War soldiers are buried at Finn's Point. There are also thirteen graves, each marked with a marble tombstone, of World War II German Army POWs who were among the thousands brought to the United States, fifty-four of whom were commanded to work at New Jersey's army base, Fort Dix, aiding the American war effort. The thirteen died while in captivity, three by hanging themselves from the rafters of their room after a riot on June 28, 1945. The tombstones of the three all bear the same date, June 29, 1945.

As suggested earlier, I remember feeling somewhat uncomfortable as I looked over the cemetery, muttering to myself, "Confederates are bad enough, but Nazis? Can't we do better in a New Jersey cemetery?" Actually, though it has long been assumed all thirteen were Germans, those buried there are a strange lot. Some with typically Slavic names were Russians who had joined German forces in their escape from Stalinist Russia. It is generally believed that the riot was the result of these men being informed that they would be repatriated to the Soviet Union the next day, where they expected to face certain torture before being executed. During the rebellion, some begged their American guards to shoot them dead. Some, who became violent, were indeed severely wounded but did not die immediately. The dates of death of three others are early July, suggesting that they must have succumbed to their wounds in the days following the riot. One mystery is that alongside the nooses of the three who hanged themselves were fifteen others. Who had intended to use them remains a mystery, but it is likely that other Russian Nazi soldiers had decided to hang themselves but either didn't get the chance, perhaps because they were shot in the riot, or changed their minds.

It is something of an error to call Finn's Point a New Jersey cemetery. It was declared a national cemetery in 1875, one of 155 spread across 42 states and Puerto Rico. So, while few northern states would welcome having these bodies in its cemetery, and the Fort Delaware Confederates all died in what is technically Delaware, state borders are not considered in locating appropriate national burial sites. For those of us, myself included, who may have believed that Arlington National Cemetery, just across the Potomac from Washington, DC, was *the* national cemetery for deceased soldiers, the fact that there are 155 national cemeteries for veterans may be something of a revelation. Arlington is managed by the United States Army, the other 154 by the Veteran's Administration. New Jersey has two of them: Finn's Point and one in Beverly, New Jersey, in Burlington County, now considered at full capacity. There is also a state created and managed veteran's cemetery in Hanover Township, also in Burlington County. Though they are eligible to be buried there it is unlikely that veterans of our wars would choose to be buried at Finn's Point, given most of the other occupants of the cemetery, and I did not see any graves of World War I or World War II American casualties at Finn's Point.

Most New Jerseyans have never heard of the Finn's Point cemetery. But on May 9, 1997, it entered the news in a dramatic fashion. A serial killer, Andrew Cunanan, who had already murdered three other men and was on his way to Florida, happened to stop at the Finn's Point cemetery. His stolen car was failing and he wanted a well-functioning vehicle. In the caretaker's house he encountered and killed the caretaker William Reece on May 9 in order to steal his red pickup truck. While the media paid scant attention to this atrocity, shortly after Cunanan arrived in Miami he murdered the world-famous Italian fashion designer Gianni Versace on July 15.

Versace spent part of each year in the South Beach area of Miami and, indeed, was credited (partly for his creation of a magnificent mansion) with making South Beach fashionable. He was seen as its unofficial mayor. With Versace's death, and Cunanan's suicide as lawmen were closing in on a houseboat he had taken over (they had found Reece's pickup truck nearby), the story made national headlines and the Finn's Point cemetery received attention it has never known before or since.

Finn's Point may be little known, but between being the site of unusual burials, to say the least, and the murder that took place there, it is regarded by some as haunted. I spoke with a woman in the nearby town of Pennsville who told me she has never gone there and never will. "It's haunted!" she said. "Everyone knows that." If any cemetery is haunted, Finn's Point would be the one. Haunted or not, Finn's Point was placed on the National Register of Historic Places in 1978.

The Delaware Water Gap and the Old Mine Road

The Delaware Water Gap

The Delaware Water Gap may well be New Jersey's grandest sight. The river forms an elegant S-curve at the end of the Kittatinny Mountains and between Mount Tammany on the New Jersey side of the Delaware and Mount Minsi on the Pennsylvania side. You can see, and almost feel, how the water clawed its way down through the rock over the centuries. It's not the Grand Canyon, but it is more accessible and has its own special and dramatic charms. Both mountains are reasonably easy to climb, and from above they present a totally different perspective on the Gap—though canoeing through the Gap or observing it at water level, for instance at the Kittatinny Point Visitor Center, off Interstate 80 just before it crosses into Pennsylvania, can be equally intriguing. The visitor center is, by the way, the southernmost place where you can put your canoe or kayak into the water and still be just inside the Delaware Water Gap, but there are plenty of other places upstream and it would make more sense to put in at one of those and paddle down through the Gap with the current.

Inside the Delaware Water Gap.

Being alongside or on the river and staring up at the surrounding mountains is exciting. Even better: if you climb either mountain in late spring you will be all but encased in rhododendron and mountain laurel groves, now in bloom, the most abundant I have ever witnessed. It's worth climbing up there for the flowers alone. The leaf colors in fall are also extraordinary. All the seasons in the Gap seem to have a special quality of their own. The early name of the Gap was Paradise Valley, and when you are there the name seems entirely appropriate.

The Gap lends its name to the Delaware Water Gap National Recreation Area, which extends north from the Gap along the river for forty-seven miles.[1] The 70,000-acre recreation area, shared by New Jersey and Pennsylvania, was created by Congress when efforts to build a dam six miles upriver at Tocks Island failed after years of controversy. Had the dam been built, the waters would have covered at least forty of those miles with a great lake obscuring both the New Jersey and Pennsylvania sides of the river, obliterating a multitude of historic houses, stores, and hamlets as well as Native American historic sites and burial grounds.

If that dam had been built, all the beauty of the river itself for those many miles would have been sacrificed. It would have been one big blob of water, all the variety and history gone. For example, the charm of the Wallpack

Bend, ten miles upriver from the Gap, would have been no more. This bend is so unique it actually has the river running north for a while until it rights itself and continues south. That huge lake would have covered up the bend and the magnificent terrain it passes through and many other incomparable sights.

Also, trapped by a dam the water would not have been as pure as it is in a free-flowing river surrounded by mountains and trees and lovely trails that guide you through it all. There is also a magnificent collection of waterfalls coming down from the heights on both sides of the Delaware to join it below. Buttermilk Falls on the New Jersey side, tumbling from rock to rock for 200 feet, is delicate but actually the highest waterfall in the state—and the prettiest. I say this with due respect for the powerful Paterson Falls of the Passaic in Paterson. Turning the upper Delaware into a giant lake would have been a pity for many reasons, but one would have been its obscuring of the lower parts of a number of glorious waterfalls.

There is a movement afoot to get Congress to declare the Gap recreation area a national park. That would be a fine idea in most people's estimation but involve one significant change: hunting is not allowed in national parks. However, this could be remedied by creating a national park and reserve, the reserve being available for hunting, as is the case with many national parks. Indeed, there is already a name for such a park being considered: the Delaware Water Gap National Recreation Area would become the Delaware Water Gap National Park and Lenape Reserve. It would also be worthwhile, and about time, to include and honor indigenous people in the naming of a national park.

I might add that there is not a single national park in the states of New York, New Jersey, Pennsylvania, or Delaware, the states that border the Delaware River, only a number of historic parks, recreation areas, and historic sites. There are sixty-three national parks, but none nearby for the people of New Jersey and the other three states. One might ask, "Why are virtually all national parks in the western United States?" And since the Gap and the lands north of it and along the river are visited each year by some 4.5 million people, more than visit many national parks in the West (including Yellowstone and the Grand Canyon) the reason for no national park is not lack of interest. Indeed, it is already estimated that the area brings in some $225 million in revenue to nearby businesses, and a national park would almost certainly increase that figure. John Donohue, for fourteen years superintendent of the Delaware Water Gap National Recreation Area and currently with the Sierra Club, said at one point during his park tenure, "This place, basically, already is a national park. The only difference between it and the national parks is the size of our budget compared with theirs." Donohue added, "This would be a dream to see this place recognized and receive the prestige it deserves."[2]

John Kashwick, vice chair of the New Jersey Sierra Club, says that "It's not just scenery. Its proximity to large urban centers like New York and Philadelphia makes it accessible to millions. It's a social justice issue. There are so many people who could be served by this site if it was a national park."[3]

Not everyone feels this way. As we will learn, thousands of people lost their homes through eminent domain in the interest of creating a dam that was never built just upriver from the Gap. They have an understandable mistrust of the federal government. "There's a lot of hard feelings around here," says Sandy Hull of Sandyston Township. Hull is a member of an association of citizens dedicated to "no national park." They call themselves The Delaware Water Gap Defense Fund and wish to protect the area "from further assaults."[4]

There are also strong feelings among hunters who have been able, in season, to hunt throughout the Gap Recreation Area and would be confined to the relatively smaller reserve area of the national park. So, there is a struggle between environmentalists and those who would relish a national park in our area of the country and others, especially those with a long memory for what they consider, with some justification, mistreatment by the federal government.

Today's struggle over the Delaware Water Gap would have been meaningless in the past when it was one of the premier resort sites in the United States, with the two sides of the river sporting forty hotels, some quite sizeable. There were also cabins and bed and breakfasts and restaurants, and even towns with trains reaching them from New York and Philadelphia. There were trolleys (horse-drawn, then electric) connecting the hotels and towns. A train from New York City crossed the Delaware where Interstate 80 crosses it today. While its first hotel was built as early as 1829, the Gap's popularity, especially among honeymooners and young families, was greatest in the six decades after the Civil War when as many as one million people vacationed there in summer.

Several of the hotels that once graced the Gap were large and grew larger with time. The Kittatinny House Hotel, first built in 1841, eventually had room for 275 guests. Added to again, it had room for 500. President Teddy

Roosevelt arrived for a short visit in 1910. Fred Astaire vacationed there with his family at fourteen. There is a short but lovely documentary readers may want to google, titled *Mountain Paradise: The Golden Era of the Delaware Water Gap* (2005), which focuses as much on the elegant life in the hotels and towns as on the beauties of the Gap itself. Another testimony to the appeal of those bygone times is a whole book that is nothing but a collection of postcards of the Gap and its hotels and little towns that were sent out to friends and family.[5]

Today there is no sign of the resort hotels in the Gap. Automobiles once traveled there, but with the arrival of the Great Depression, the old wooden hotels lost business, were abandoned, and were torn or burned down. One can come across bits of foundations and chimneys in the woods that have grown around them, but otherwise there is no sign of the festive life that once was a chief feature of these woods and mountains. For those of us who love the Gap in its present condition, which is also its original condition, it is just as well. There would not have been a national recreation area had things continued as they were—not to mention the growing possibility of a national park. The Gap and its surroundings have returned to nature, and that is worthy of celebration.

It is peaceful and lovely down in the Gap, but just as much fun to climb the mountains that surround it. They're both rounded like giant hills instead of jagged peaks and are reasonably modest climbs on well-marked trails. On top you see the Gap from a totally different perspective. Mount Tammany is a bit higher (1,526 ft. to Mount Minsi's 1,461) but the trail is less challenging—mostly just an upward walk through a forest; Minsi is rockier. Minsi also offers better views of the Gap at a variety of spots all the way up, several just off the trail.

However, especially on a hot summer day, there is a reward at the base of Tammany: the beautiful Dunnfield Creek, with its cascades of little waterfalls, some so gentle you can sit under them and feel yourself become part of the creek. I did it once with a nephew with whom I regularly hike. We could have stayed there forever. On another occasion I came down from Tammany and passed a small group of people skinny-dipping in the creek. There was something idyllic about them that added to the beauty of the creek and its surroundings. I imagined they had never felt so free. They waved to me and I waved back.

I had just come down from Tammany on a summer day a year later when I encountered a fellow in the creek and we got into conversation. I didn't have a bathing suit or I'd have joined him. When he came out, he told me he was an Appalachian Trail thru-hiker from Virginia. He was recently divorced and was hiking the long trail "to get my mind and body attached again." He had started atop Mount Katahdin in Maine in early spring and was planning to make it to Springer Mountain, Georgia, before the next winter arrived there. He was a little off the A.T. (as it is generally referred to) but had heard of Dunnfield Creek and didn't want to miss a chance to cool off and get clean.

I told him my name and asked him his. "Drumbeat Joe," he said. Seeing I was puzzled, he said, "Everyone on the trail takes on a different moniker. They either pick it themselves or someone names them. Early on the trip I was sitting alone on a boulder in Maine by the trail, tapping it with both hands while I sang a song just for fun (I love to sing out-of-doors) and some hikers came along and said, 'Well, here's Drumbeat Joe.' And that was that. Ever since, I meet people on the trail and they've heard of 'Drumbeat Joe.' It's cool. You're on this long, long trail, mostly all alone, but you and everyone else hiking it are in this club, temporary but unforgettable."

Drumbeat Joe didn't volunteer his real name and I thought it best not to inquire. He probably wouldn't have given it to me anyway. He was Drumbeat Joe, and that's all there was to it.

Drumbeat told me as he approached New Jersey heading south the trail had taken him alongside Greenwood Lake, which is in both New York State and New Jersey. Then it had turned west, hugging the New Jersey–New York border, "embroidering it," he said. "One minute I'm in New York, the next in New Jersey. I felt like skipping state-to-state along the border. In fact, I did, a little worried that someone would come along and think I was nuts." Now completely in New Jersey, he had particularly enjoyed the beauty of Sunfish Pond, the southernmost glacial tarn in New Jersey, which is some six miles above the Delaware. At that part of Dunnfield Creek, we were less than a mile from the river.

As he dried off and dressed, Drumbeat confessed that he was perplexed about how to cross the Delaware River when he descended to it. "The trail map shows me crossing it on Interstate 80, but that seems really dangerous." I told him I would drive him across if that didn't interfere with his goal of hiking every inch of the trail, currently listed, he said, at 2,193 miles. "Currently," he explained, because the trail is often slightly recalibrated based on local conditions or problems requiring slight modifications or improvements.

We located the A.T.—not easy to spot in the thick woods—and I enjoyed hiking a short way with Drumbeat, partly so I could feel that I too had been on that white-spotted trail, though I've been on chunks of it, here and there, all my life, including atop Mount Washington in New Hampshire, its second-highest point. Still, I've always been a little jealous of those who have hiked or are now hiking the whole thing. When I'm reincarnated, that's the first thing I'm going to do.

Locating my car in the little lot at the base of the trail in New Jersey, I drove Drumbeat across the river—though it proved unnecessary. There was a walkway on the bridge (unusual for an interstate), probably put there precisely for A.T. hikers, though I've always felt no bridge should be built without a safe pathway for hikers, bikers, and roller skaters. Better still would be two paths, one in each direction. On Drumbeat's instructions, I took the first exit off the bridge, Route 611. I pulled over and we both got out. Drumbeat gave me a hug. We were friends now, but it saddened me a bit to know we'd probably never see each other again.

In September I was back in the Gap planning to climb Mount Minsi on the Pennsylvania side, which Drumbeat was going to do after we parted and which I had never done before. But before I got there, I passed through a tiny town with the improbable name Delaware Water Gap, Pennsylvania, which has jazz festivals from time to time. Folks there told me that the Deer Head Inn is the oldest existing jazz club in America. I'd have thought it would be in New Orleans.

Anyway, I drove past the jazz club en route to the base of Mount Minsi, where there is a small dirt parking lot for those intent on climbing it. I went there early on a Monday morning assuming it would be a nice quiet day on the mountain. It turned out I got the last available parking space. Many people, even on a non-holiday weekday, were climbing Minsi and immersing themselves in its beauty and that of its surroundings. Actually, part of me was glad they were there. With plenty of people I wouldn't have to worry about bears.

The climb up Mount Minsi, unlike that of Mount Tammany, includes a chunk of the Appalachian Trail, so you're even more likely to run into A.T. hikers there than on the Mount. Tammany side, where I had met Drumbeat Joe just off the trail. It's always fun to meet up with thru-hikers. Contrary to what you'd imagine, they don't tend to be solitary types. Possibly due to being entirely alone for days at a time, they're eager to talk and share their adventures. One guy told me he was doing the trail for the second time, the first time south to north, this time north to south. He was seventy-two years old and seemed saddened that he probably would not be able to do it again but said he might still try. "I don't think I could survive doing it again," he said. "Then again, what better way to die?"

I asked him if he knew Drumbeat Joe.

"Sure," he replied. "We hung out for a while passing through Massachusetts."[6]

The views at several points on the way up Minsi were outstanding. At the turnouts in the trail there was little or no vegetation blocking the Gap. Hearing the A.T. hikers ooh and aah over the Gap made me wonder whether this was one of the best parts of their six-month hike. One of the A.T. hikers seemed to confirm this. "This is truly gorgeous," he told me. Unlike A.T. hikers, I hadn't tramped over hundreds of miles of mountains and through thick woods to get there, but the views were so beautiful I dropped the jealousy I felt toward them, realizing that I could go to the Gap and climb Mount Minsi any time I desired.

I've climbed a lot of mountains, but Minsi is special. Every hundred yards or so a stream runs right over the trail. You go from rock to rock—carefully.

The Delaware Water Gap in fall, shot from a height on Mt. Minsi. Mt. Tammany (and the New Jersey side) is on the left.

I did fine on the way up, but was so tired on the way down I was afraid of falling and just walked through the shallow rivers. That was fun, actually, something I'd never done before. It may not be good for your shoes, but it's a present to your soul.

In my car I removed my shoes and socks and drove home barefoot. Someone once told me that's against the law. If it is, that's ridiculous. I think we're more in control of our cars barefoot than with any kind of footgear. At least that's what I planned to tell the cop when I was ticketed for driving barefoot.

The Old Mine Road

If the Gap and the mountains weren't enough to interest adventurers, there's the Old Mine Road running alongside the river on the New Jersey side, beginning in the Gap and continuing all the way north through the state. It is believed to be the oldest wheeled vehicle road of any length in America.[7] To get there, you take Exit 1 off Interstate 80 just before it crosses the Delaware. In the days of the Lenape Indians it was a forest path, but the Dutch widened it into a dirt road in the seventeenth century to get out precious mined copper.

The Old Mine Road, 104 miles in total, continues in New Jersey for some 42 miles and then, near Port Jervis, makes an abrupt right turn and continues on to Kingston, New York, on the Hudson River. The last 60 miles of the road is, today, a modern highway. The Dutch also found some silver in those mines. But the mineral harvesting of both silver and copper, proved so scarce over time that the mines were abandoned. Some of the Dutch decided to live in Kingston, while others settled down along the Old Mine Road, building houses and farming the rich soil that frames the Delaware River as it does the floodplain of every river.

Up on the hills bordering the road are remnants of partially collapsed holes Dutch miners left in the forest. You approach them carefully because they're readymade to serve as bears' lairs, and you'd better not enter any of them. Attacks by bears are rare; they are usually more afraid of us than we are of them. But if you enter their homes, you're in serious trouble. In 2014 a Rutgers University student hiking in North Jersey was killed by a bear.

The mine area was called Pahaquarry, derived from the Lenape word *pahaqualog*, which roughly translated means "side of the mountain near the water." Indeed, the mines are on the western side of the Kittatinny Mountains. One mine hole I approached gave me some assurance by having iron bars across its entrance, so I went right up to it and peered in with my flashlight. It was difficult to see how far in it went. There are eighteen mine openings, and some believe the longest extends 500 feet, but this was something I was unable, and afraid, to ascertain.

The Old Mine Road is narrow, so you have to be alert to occasional vehicles coming the other way. They're so few everyone slows and waves, like it's a big deal to encounter someone else on this road, almost a cause for celebration. The road can handle two-lane traffic but only if everyone slows way down (there are signs along it requesting a speed of fifteen miles per hour throughout). It's full of potholes and history. On a weekday the traffic is scarce to nonexistent, which is welcome—though one might also ask, "What do I do if my car breaks down or runs out of gas? Could Triple A find me here? Even *I* don't know where I am!"

Along the road, especially in the south, are abandoned houses and hamlets, falling apart and crumbling, with trees growing out of them and vines pulling them apart. In some cases all that remains are the foundations of

A home along the Old Mine Road left in unrecoverable condition by the Army Corps of Engineers, the trees growing out of the house accelerating its return to nature.

houses and settlements. There are also small family cemeteries and the remains of driveways that lead to nothing discernible.

It wasn't always this way. William Henry Harrison lived for some years with his family in a home along the Old Mine Road. Perhaps he should have stayed there. Elected president of the United States in 1841, he caught a cold that turned into pneumonia after he delivered a lengthy inaugural address on a freezing day. When he died, he had been in office a total of only thirty-two days, virtually all spent in bed.

Earlier, John Adams rode horseback on the Old Mine Road on a trip from Boston to Philadelphia to attend Congress, stopping at the Van Campen Inn, built around 1750, which is still just off the road, a beautiful stone building and national historic site.

You feel like an explorer on this road, especially when observing the plentiful signs warning of the presence of bears on the one hand and timber rattlesnakes and northern copperheads on the other. I didn't see a bear or any snakes, but a tribe of wild turkeys, twenty at least, brought me to a complete stop as they slowly crept across the road, acting as if they owned it, which I suppose they did more than I. They lived there; I was just passing through. One refused to get off the road. I honked my horn, but he kept looking at me as if to say, "Who the hell are you?" His buddies watched from the sidelines. To pass him, I had to drive up on the leaves and mud and sticks on the right side of the road, praying that I wasn't going into a ditch.

It's hard to remember that all of this extraordinary abundance of nature, the Gap and forest and the turkeys and the Old Mine Road, is in New Jersey, the most densely populated of the fifty states. However, there are still vast sections as pretty as the special places other states feature, and they are prettier than most. Out by the Gap and the Old Mine Road, New Jersey might well be called the Nature State. Given its beauty and variety, the state seems to have more important things to do these days than feeding New York and Philadelphia, which was once a key function, partially justifying the moniker the Garden State.

Just opposite where I was traveling was Minisink Island, where the Munsee tribe of the Lenape once had a major village. What better security than building your town on an island in the middle of a river—which the Dutch also did on Burlington Island. Another aspect of the Old Mine Road worth noting is its role in both the French and Indian War and the Revolutionary War. While Native Americans had gotten along reasonably well with Dutch settlers, who treated them with respect, they did not trust the British, who seemed intent on taking all their lands and, if so inclined, cheating them. There was an incident, apocryphal but based on an actual treaty, called "Penn's Walk," in which William Penn made a deal to buy as much land as his sons could walk in three days, a procedure stipulated by the Native Americans. After a day and a half Penn felt that he had sufficient land. But his sons kept going for three days, and they didn't walk; they ran as fast as they could and kept going through the night. It was the beginning of mistrust of the English by the Native peoples of the region.[8]

While we often think of the French and Indian War as taking place in northern New York State (partly under the influence of James Fenimore Cooper's novels) there was considerable fighting in New Jersey, especially along the Old Mine Road, with the Lenapes fighting on the French side. Eight forts or fortified houses were built along the road where settlers would gather when they felt endangered.

The Native Americans were more neutral during the Revolutionary War. The Americans and British fought more than a few skirmishes and even a battle along the Old Mine Road. To join George Washington for the first Battle of Trenton, a contingent of the Continental Army marched down the Old Mine Road along which they had been stationed and then, finding boats, sailed the rest of the way, arriving too late to join him.

Casimir Pulaski, a Pole who had joined the American forces and was made a general after he had steered Washington and his troops out of a sure British trap, was sent with 600 men to guard against British advances from the north along the Old Mine Road. Pulaski was killed in a battle near Savannah, Georgia, in 1779. He was an enthusiastic practitioner of fighting on horseback and is regarded to this day as the Father of the American Cavalry. The 3.5-mile Pulaski Skyway, which bridges the Passaic and Hackensack Rivers and the marshes between Newark and Jersey City, is named for him. Recent evidence suggests that Pulaski may have actually been a woman or a transgender individual—long before the concept of gender being on a spectrum had become common knowledge as it has in our times.[9]

I relished my trip along the Old Mine Road. It was a trip back in time, a way of visiting a world centuries old. When I completed the New Jersey part near Port Jervis, New York, I got on a speeding highway to head home, realizing belatedly that the highway had once been the Old Mine Road where it turns toward Kingston. I missed the part of the road back along the Delaware and wished I was still on it. It took a while to get used to traveling sixty-five miles an hour after traveling fifteen. Going fifteen instead of sixty-five once in a while might be a metaphor for living a less anxious and more purposeful life. Going fifteen you can better enjoy every inch of the terrain and feel, even in an automobile, that you are part of the land.

5

The Dam That Was Never Built

In earlier chapters I described places or issues concerning the Delaware River as a whole. In this chapter I will be discussing something concerning the river that *didn't* happen. The Tocks Island Dam controversy was one of the great events in the river's history and it went on for forty years. As well, it affirmed a new way of thinking about the environment that has had wide applications elsewhere in America and around the world. Increasingly we are hearing the argument that nature has intrinsic rights, just like people.

Dams may be necessary in places of great drought such as the American Southwest, where the Hoover Dam outside Las Vegas, for example, conserves every ounce of the Colorado River, to be distributed as needed. But New Jersey is a well-watered state that need hardly concern itself with drought and even seems to be getting wetter with climate change.

The Tocks Island Dam project arose after the 1955 flood, the greatest Delaware River Basin flood in recorded history.[1] It was the result of back-to-back hurricanes that August, Diane following immediately in the footsteps of Connie. Ninety-nine people died in the Delaware Valley. Property damage was $100 million. Some of the Delaware's bridges were torn off their moorings, including the last of the sixteen covered bridges that once spanned the river, the Columbia, New Jersey, to Portland, Pennsylvania, bridge. In a flood, a covered bridge is a perfect target. It is solid but lightweight and does not allow water to pass through it as a steel bridge would. A covered bridge is basically a wooden box. When smacked by a wall of water it is likely to just float away. But the 1955 flood was so monumental it even tore up some steel bridges, or after dislodging them sent them downriver to crash into and wreck other bridges.

Immediately following the hurricanes, a cry arose to build a dam that would prevent future floods, and Tocks Island, some six miles north of the Delaware Water Gap, was suggested as the best site. The controversy over whether to actually build the dam extended from the early 1960s through 2002. In 1962, Congress passed a bill approving the dam, and President Kennedy signed the legislation. The money was yet to be appropriated, but the Army Corps of Engineers began its work immediately. Then all hell broke loose.[2]

A dam is considered by environmentalists contrary to nature, specifically the beauty of a free-flowing river. And this dam would have created a deep lake many miles long behind it, obliterating many miles of the river but also its beautiful surroundings, including countless historic houses and other buildings. The dam would also drown all of the Old Mine Road north of it. By limiting the river to a fraction of its normal flow, it would have not only reduced its availability for recreation but also negatively affected fish and other wildlife, as well as people.

This would have also been true below Trenton, where the mixture of fresh and tidal salt water that is perfect for certain spawning species, especially sturgeon, would now be altered so as to be much more exclusively salt water. Silt and pernicious substances of all kinds would have backed up behind the dam, and reeds and marshes would have grown in what had been clean, flowing water, making the river beyond the dam murky and less supportive of the species it had long fostered—shad for example, and, farther south, especially in the bay, oysters. Shad would simply not be able to get to their spawning grounds further upriver and would die out.

Not to mention the impact the dam would have on our own species. When one considers that the Delaware River contributes to the drinking water of some seventeen million people (including residents of New York City and Philadelphia), not maintaining its healthfulness at the highest level would have had pernicious effects on human health. Relatively still water in lakes is more conducive to parasites and chemicals, which are concentrated and made more pernicious because they cannot easily be dispersed by the river's current, not the equal of free-flowing river water in terms of purity. Also, the less chlorine you have to add to drinking water, the healthier and tastier it is to drink.

A considerable number of the ninety-nine deaths in the 1955 flood of the Delaware Basin were not from the Delaware itself but its tributaries. Forty were mostly women and children vacationing in cabins near Broadhead Creek, a tributary close to the town of Analomink, Pennsylvania. The rain was so torrential, and accumulated so rapidly, there was no escape. The creek rose to thirty feet, smashing the cabins or simply carrying them into the Delaware River.

This was similar to what happened on September 1, 2021, when Hurricane Ida struck New Jersey. Of the thirty deaths in the state, none were from the Delaware itself, nor were the many millions in property damage caused by the river. It was the Delaware's tributaries, well over 200 creeks converted to watery monsters. Creeks usually originate in high areas like mountains and hills, and when swollen they run downhill with considerable force. This was particularly true in Lambertville, which suffered massive damage, the water running down from the high hills just east of it, the worst flooding in its recorded history.

The Delaware River did not rise sufficiently to enter the town. The damage was caused by three small tributaries, Swan Creek, Ely Creek, and Alexauken Creek, whose courses run on the south, middle, and north sides of town, respectively. They are normally mere trickles but were swollen in just a few hours by eleven inches of rain. Ely normally runs under the town in a culvert and into the Delaware, but it burst, swamping a multitude of houses. As for the other two creeks, twenty-foot-high mountains of water poured down from the high hills east of the town. On the hill where Alexauken Creek originates, a housing project had been built not long before that helped swell the creek. A multitude of trees were taken down to build the project, greatly reducing the ability of the land to absorb water. Great quantities of water poured from the buildings and paving of that project, including its parking lots; much of it might have been absorbed had the project not been built on a hill overlooking the town or had conveyances been built to take the water elsewhere.

Charlie Groth, whom I mentioned in the discussion of the Shad Fishery on Lewis Island in Chapter 3, and whose home sustained considerable damage from Alexauken Creek, wrote to me: "Redirecting streams has been on the table and off . . . again and again. Perhaps now it will be *on*." But it seems

The power of tributaries however small: a house wrecked and pushed off its foundation by Swann Creek in Lambertville, normally a trickle but turned into a wall of water by Hurricane Ida on September 1, 2021. A few days later, Swann Creek was again a trickle.

to me extraordinary that one has to consider redirecting streams that are hardly more than brooks, an example of how tributaries of any size can do considerable damage.

By late April of 2022, eight months after Hurricane Ida, she had still not been able to move back into her home. Elsewhere in town work on only half of the 287 public projects needing repair had been initiated or completed a year after Ida. One of these was the planting of a multitude of trees wherever flooding might be expected in the future. There seems to be an indomitable spirit among river people. Despite all the destruction, examined by Governor Murphy in a visit to Lambertville, signs sprung up around town saying LAMBERTVILLE, WHERE OUR COMEBACK WILL BE STRONGER THAN OUR SETBACK.

Tributaries can be as important as major rivers, and sometimes more so during floods. Indeed, while many organizations concern themselves with the Delaware as a whole, others focus on a particular tributary, for example the Musconetcong Watershed Association. Thus, the question arises: Much as people love living alongside flowing water, is it in the best interest of society for rivers to be crippled by dams, or should people simply reside farther away from waterways?

This was a question on the mind of Tracy Carluccio, deputy director of the Delaware Riverkeeper Network, when I interviewed her. From the point of view of the Riverkeeper Network, the river should always come first, and its natural state should be protected. "Trees and their elaborate root systems stop floods as successfully as do dams and at no cost to the environment," Carluccio said. Thus, logging should never be done close to rivers or their tributaries. The Riverkeeper Network is one of some ten organizations passionately dedicated to keeping the Delaware running smoothly and clean, even if occasionally a price must be paid. One can be certain the American Rivers organization would not have named the Delaware 2020's "River of the Year" if the Tocks Island Dam had been built.

Is it not ultimately in our interest, and do we not owe it to our descendants, to maintain in their natural state rivers such as the Delaware, with its beauty, adventure, and other gifts to the human spirit, at whatever cost? This question has become more urgent with the advent of climate change and rising sea levels, so it is just as relevant on the Atlantic shore as it is on the Delaware. Is it society's responsibility when people knowingly put themselves in danger by living close to the water, primarily to enjoy the view? No one is proposing tearing down houses already built on the river or coast, but should society prohibit new housing in such areas or, at least, wash its hands off any further support, financial and otherwise, for such projects when they are damaged or destroyed?

These were among the questions an environmental movement concerning the Delaware, at first very small, would slowly feed upon. A few principled individuals wished to protect the prettiest part of the Delaware River and its surroundings from being covered by a giant lake. In addition, they argued that the proposed dam and the geology of Tock's Island would be unstable, citing examples of dams built elsewhere in the same fashion and on similar terrain that had collapsed, one being the Teton Dam, which held back a quantity of water much smaller than the Tocks Island Dam would have contained. The Army Corps of Engineers had already drilled down 140 feet on the island and not come upon bedrock. What they encountered was unstable glacial material. If a Tocks Island Dam gave way the results would have been catastrophic. The mountain of water would have caused untold deaths and the destruction of towns and other property of a magnitude far beyond what an undammed Delaware was capable of in a worst-case scenario—the 1955 flood being an example.

The Tocks Island project also would have involved the utilization of the beautiful and beloved Sunfish Pond, six miles above the Delaware River along the Appalachian Trail. It would have been greatly enlarged from its forty-four acres and industrialized into a subsidiary reservoir and power-generating station, precluding its function as a site of particular beauty for hikers coming from the Delaware or Appalachian Trail, perhaps completing their final New Jersey miles. The State of New Jersey had sold the pond to the development company charged by the Army Corps of Engineers with this task. The proposed ruination of Sunfish Pond caused others to join the Save the Delaware movement, including figures of statewide and even national stature.

Especially helpful were the efforts of Supreme Court Justice William O. Douglas, who, in 1967, participated in a climb up to Sunfish Pond with 600 people. Said Douglas, "Sunfish Pond is a unique spot and deserves to be preserved." Two years later he got his wish. The pond, which had been sold by the state to the company preparing to turn it into a reservoir, was sold back to the state and a year later placed on the Registry of National Landmarks. Justice Douglas followed his mild statement with one of a different nature. "The Army Corps of Engineers is public enemy number one," he said.[3]

Another public figure who contributed was New Jersey Governor Brendan Byrne, soon to be celebrated for sponsoring environmental projects, including, in 1974, the linear seventy-mile Delaware and Raritan Canal State Park, comprising the canal itself, its mule towpath, and its immediate surroundings. Byrne was also instrumental in fostering the Pine Barrens Protection Act, which prohibited any further development in that vast, virtually unpopulated part of the state, whose sandy land and stunted woodlands are coursed by sweet little rivers. Canoeing there, thirsty folks often drink the water right out of such rivers as the Mullica and don't get sick. I can personally attest to this. What a triumph in a small state with an enormous number of Superfund projects! Also, underlying the Pine Barrens is a one-hundred-square-mile lake of the purest water on the planet, rainwater filtered by the sand that has accumulated since time immemorial, a resource upon which we may someday wish to draw. If called upon, this underground lake could take care of all the freshwater needs of Philadelphia or cities of like size.

The Delaware, the state park, and the Pine Barrens have always been choice spots for hiking, camping, biking, or canoeing. As for the Tocks Island Dam, Byrne participated in a "canoe-in" at Tocks Island in 1974. Many in the canoes held signs that brought considerable attention to the Save the Delaware movement. More than any governor, Byrne's efforts reduced New Jersey's longtime reputation of pollution and its often-attendant political corruption.

One may wonder why the Army Corps has been such a target of disdain. During World War II it was celebrated as instrumental to America's victory. The American military would attack and take over a Pacific island held by the Japanese. Immediately, the Corps would be commanded to build an airplane landing strip—in twenty-four hours if possible—so as to put American bombers in closer proximity to Japan and make roundtrip flights there possible. To their great credit, they did it. It was the same with instant bridges in the European Theatre, since the originals were destroyed by retreating Nazis.

Immediate productivity was inherent in how the New Jersey Turnpike was built in a year and a half early in the 1950s. The leadership of the project were some of the same people, or people with the same ideology, as those who had built airstrips and bridges overnight during the war. Their motto was, "Just do it!" While getting things done as quickly as possible without public discussion may have its virtues in wartime or in times of emergency, this was a domestic project, and Americans affected by it might have wanted some say from an environmental and quality of life perspective. Instead, the Turnpike was built right down the middle of the City of Elizabeth. No one was consulted, and it had a major negative effect on the city's viability and vitality. The Turnpike got built—and incredibly fast—but could it not, with a little thought, have been built less intrusively, with more greenery in its northern stretches and with at least some concern for aesthetics?

With the Tocks Island Dam project, the Army Corps proceeded in like fashion. Continuing to assume the funding of the dam, they used the principle of eminent domain when riverside residents would not leave on their own, which was virtually all of them. A total of 8,000 people were removed from their homes on both sides of the river—including people whose families, in many cases, had lived in these homes for hundreds of years. Sometimes the Corps wanted people's farmland rather than their homes, which would leave them with homes but no livelihood. Other times it was the homes the Corps wanted and not the land, so people could farm, but where would they live? Sometimes, to convince residents that remaining where they were was hopeless, the Corps removed road access to homes. The Corps reasoned that none of this would matter: both the lands and the homes would eventually be covered by water when the dam was built.

When their properties were condemned, homeowners were paid what they considered a pittance compared to their true value—not to mention their historic, aesthetic, and personal value—and when they would not leave willingly the Corps arrived with bulldozers anyway. At public meetings there was a good deal of shouting and not a few who cried. Some carried signs that read:

NO MORE SHAD

OYSTERS, FARMS, FORESTS

EAT AN ENGINEER FOR LUNCH TOMORROW

NIX ON TOCKS.[4]

One man who was removed from his home was elderly and blind. Another committed suicide. Some threatened to shoot anyone who came near their homes with the intent of destroying them. Others vowed that Corps members who approached their homes would be lynched. These things never happened, but in their rage the homeowners inadvertently became part of the environmental forces opposing the dam.

At this point the courts issued a restraining order prohibiting the destruction of any more houses until the project was indeed financially bankrolled by Congress. But if the Army Corps of Engineers had not sufficiently antagonized homeowners, they now went further. They put "For Rent" advertisements in New York newspapers. They intended to rent out still intact houses as a way of raising funds. This was nothing short of spitting in the faces of the former owners. They had been paid little and forced to seek shelter elsewhere, and now others were invited to reside in their homes.

Many of these others were not typical. An army of hippies moved into the homes, many too impoverished to pay the rent demanded of them. The Army Corps began to consider the hippies squatters; they called themselves "river people" or "cloud farmers." They had come from the cities with hopes of living off the land. Music and marijuana, the latter still totally illegal, pervaded the air. Both sides of the river were turned into mini Woodstocks. Indeed, Abbie Hoffman of Woodstock and Chicago Seven fame joined the hippies for some time. One woman provided evidence of an alternative lifestyle by routinely shopping in nearby towns completely nude.

Eventually the Army Corps of Engineers, aided on both sides of the river by the state police of New Jersey and Pennsylvania, raided the squatters' camps and physically removed their occupants. One woman who had given birth hours before was forced to walk away from her temporary riverside home carrying her newborn infant. The Corps did not allow the hippies time to gather their possessions or even to take or make arrangements for their pets. No provisions were made for the farm animals—cows, chickens, etc.—that some of them possessed or crops that, if left unattended, would likely be overcome by weeds or otherwise wither and die. Now the Army Corps and their dam project had a whole new band of people who hated them.

Some of the evictees were kindly offered hospitality by nearby residents who, while not enthusiastic about the hippies, hated the Army Corps of Engineers and their dam project and were willing to do anything to undermine it. Now the Corps further complicated their relations with the public by seeking out previous owners of still intact houses in an attempt to rent their own houses to them, which the former homeowners regarded as yet another insult and, having settled elsewhere, all but universally turned down with disdain. As far as they knew, the Army Corps would soon be tearing down their former houses anyway. So, most houses remained empty.

On the national level, members of Congress were increasingly rethinking whether the Tocks Island Dam was a good idea. They were aided and abetted by another public figure. In 1973, while Jimmy Carter was governor of Georgia, he was outspoken in his condemnation of the project. Carter spoke of "a growing awareness of the value of . . . irreplaceable resources," an idea he would carry into his presidency. His statement came from experience. He had earlier labored to stop the building of the Sewell Bluff Dam in Georgia. And his ideas about Sewell Bluff and Tocks Island were influenced by the Army Corps' project, abandoned in 1969, of building a dam across the Red River Gorge in Kentucky.

But it was Lyndon Johnson who, inadvertently, made the project impossible. The Vietnam War was at its height and Johnson needed all the funds that could be mustered to pursue an ever-distant victory. He was emphatic that no domestic projects, unless absolutely necessary, should be funded if they would diminish resources for the war effort. The Army Corps of Engineers put the dam project on hold for an indefinite period. When the Vietnam War ended in 1975, the Corps proposed reconsidering the project, but three of the four states that border the Delaware insisted they did not want the dam. In 1977, the very section of the Delaware where the dam and the lake behind it would have been was placed by the federal government on its list of Wild and Scenic Rivers, legislation for which was passed in 1968. In 1992 the dam was considered again and more emphatically rejected. In 2002, Congress passed a bill specifically prohibiting the building of a Tocks Island Dam.

So, the Vietnam War, which killed 58,000 Americans and 2–3 million Vietnamese, and accomplished absolutely nothing of value, did help accomplish one thing: it devoured money that might have gone into building the Tocks Island Dam, which most people feel would have been another sorry mistake. And the definitive rejection of the Tocks Island Dam helped Americans to see that environmentalism was not a luxury but a necessity. It sounds ridiculous, but the Vietnam War may well have saved the Delaware River. And abandoning the Tocks Island Dam had much to do with the creation of the Delaware Water Gap Recreation Area and the likelihood that someday it may become a national park.

The reversal in dam-building would be emulated elsewhere in the country where dams were being considered and it had a major effect on movements for the removal of existing dams, as well as the environmental movement as a whole. Of course, where such dams are used to generate electricity, their removal, especially given our desire to create electricity without using fossil fuels, becomes more problematic. Indeed, despite my strong sympathies for those against the Tocks Island Dam, I sometimes wonder whether it may yet be built someday along with a host of other new dams as part of the movement to save our planet. Solar farms and solar-roofed houses are certainly unattractive. Further overcoming the natural landscape, electricity generating windmills look like the planet has been invaded as in a science fiction fantasy. Thus, a day may come when more, rather than fewer, dams will be considered essential to our survival. For the present, though, I'm delighted that there isn't one on the Delaware River.

By not building the dam, many Americans slowly came to believe that, wherever possible, protecting nature came first. Indeed, in naturalist and legal circles a movement is gaining strength that insists nature has not just moral but legal rights and that, represented by attorneys, nature may itself go to court.[5]

There is a different America emerging. Once the nation's only value regarding the environment was economic: How to make money out of it? President Herbert Hoover's 1928 statement, "Every drop of water which runs to the sea without yielding its full economic services is a waste" is an idea Americans increasingly reject.

But there remains a problem. If the survival of the planet is dependent on reducing the burning of fossil fuels, is not hydroelectric power generation, along with wind, solar, and nuclear (if it can be made definitively safe) the means to do so? Only 17 percent of rivers in Europe have no dams. Some have several dams each. The water flows through one dam, generates electric power there, and continues on to the next dam to repeat the process. Of course, these rivers have obviously sacrificed much of their beauty and water quality. Altering a river with a dam also damages irreplaceable wetlands and riparian habitats and kills wildlife. In our efforts to save the planet, should we keep so many dams in Europe as well as in the United States? Currently, in some places on both continents new dams are being constructed and in others they are being torn down. No wonder it took forty years to definitively determine not to build the Tocks Island Dam, for it was part of a larger controversy. But if mankind were to do away with dams everywhere and create more and more solar farms and windmills, is it not possible that they would come to so dominate the landscape as to create greater ugliness than the dams that mar our rivers?

America's greatest dam, the Hoover Dam outside Las Vegas, has seventeen huge water-powered generators each capable of producing enough electricity for 65,000 homes. That's a lot of electricity produced without adding to climate change by burning fossil fuels. If only it were that simple. Drought has so reduced the Colorado River, which the Hoover Dam holds back as Lake Mead, that generator intakes are beginning to appear above the water line and are thus incapable of producing electricity. If the drought occurring throughout the American Southwest in recent years is replaced by plentiful rain or the Colorado River is returned to its customary plenitude by artificial means—for example using a large pipeline from the Mississippi—the Hoover's electricity output may be returned to normal. But it will still be a giant dam in a river, something those who love rivers are anxious to avoid because of their negative effects on nature and its aesthetic beauty as well as on the quality of their water. Will we continue to take down and prevent the building of dams or will we find ourselves forced to build more of them?

Clearly, we are uncertain how to proceed. We must save the planet but hopefully not make it ugly in the process. Americans, and New Jerseyans in particular, should take particular pride in the fact that at least the Delaware River remains unmarred by dams or pollution, and we should never take our good fortune for granted. A day may yet come when we can no longer afford it.

The River and
the Canals

After discussing a dubious project on the Delaware that was never consummated, this may be a good time to discuss two worthy projects that were indeed brought to completion, the Morris Canal (1831) and the Delaware and Raritan Canal (1834)—both connected to the Delaware River. More so the Delaware and Raritan, for it begins with a twenty-two-mile feeder of Delaware River water that parallels the river and is the main water source of the canal proper, which begins in Trenton—though it could be argued that it originally began on the river in Bordentown, because that was where the heaviest laden cargo boats entered, many coming up from Philadelphia.

The Delaware and Raritan Canal might be thought of as a manmade off-shoot of the Delaware River, the Morris only so in its beginnings, though one of the major sources of its waters was the Musconetcong River, a major tributary of the Delaware. Although the Morris is less connected to the Delaware River than the Delaware and Raritan, it may be of interest to the reader to learn about both of New Jersey's canals.

On the map the two canals are presented in their original form, not as they are today. In their present form the Morris hardly exists, and experiencing it is mostly an historical enterprise. As for the Delaware and

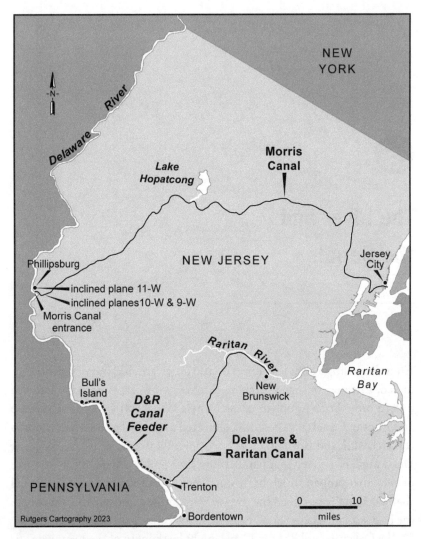

Map of New Jersey's Canals. Rutgers Cartography 2023.

Raritan, it still crosses New Jersey and mostly pours into the Raritan River three miles from where it originally did. Also, it once had a Bordentown to Trenton chunk that was abandoned. There are other changes too, so I thought it best to present a map of the canals in their original form to avoid confusion and allow me to discuss the changes in each.

New Jersey was uniquely endowed with canals, perhaps more than any other state, especially given its modest size. Besides the state's own needs, the canals served as a conduit between two great cities, New York and Philadelphia. Today, the New Jersey Turnpike is the main source of this same connection. However, the canals froze in winter, so they could not function year-round. Canal workers often earned income in winter by cutting canal ice for sale in an era before refrigerators. Preceding the world of substantial roads and modern all-weather wheeled vehicles (trains, automobiles, trucks), New Jersey was traversed by these two great canals, each carrying a variety of products, but mostly Pennsylvania's coal to New York's furnaces and in the case of the Morris considerable iron ore as well. Passing through New Jersey's iron district, the Morris Canal served to revive an industry that was suffering neglect. The district had been instrumental to the needs of George Washington's army, manufacturing cannon, cannon balls and the like during the Revolutionary War.

Canal boats commonly crossed the Delaware after emerging from canals on the Pennsylvania side. Instead of fighting the river current, the boats (ferry boats as well) often utilized it by being attached to an overhead cable that conveyed them forward on an angle leading to the entry point of the canals (or ferry docks).

Both New Jersey canals would prove to be more important economically than New York's Erie Canal (1825), in terms of the loads they carried and their contributions to industry. The Erie, however, did serve as an inspiration for the New Jersey canals. The Erie is also famed for providing transportation to Americans heading west. Leaving New York City, pioneers would first go up the Hudson, then across New York State on the canal, essentially imitating the route of today's New York Thruway. Finally, entering the Great Lakes, travelers proceeded to their respective destinations.

There could hardly be two canals less like each other than New Jersey's. The Morris was the engineering wonder of its day, the Delaware and Raritan built in a more conventional fashion. Rising from the Delaware at Phillipsburg, the river area before the entrance of the Morris merited the title Port Delaware because, with so much traffic, a basin where boats could wait their turn to enter the canal and shops providing food and other necessities for the five-day journey were key features of the port. Today there are no remaining signs of the port and the entrance to the canal is almost totally overgrow with vegetation.

The Morris traversed high hills, some rugged, until it reached the vicinity of Lake Hopatcong (earlier known as "Great Pond"). George P. Macculloch (1775–1858), for whom there is a substantial museum in what was once

The overgrown entrance to the Morris Canal on the Delaware River.

his home in Morristown, is generally credited with being the Father of the Morris Canal. Legend has it that he was fishing on Lake Hopatcong when he realized that a canal across New Jersey was desperately needed if it were to prosper, and that the waters of the lake, aided by streams, could feed it in both directions. Macculloch made a sketch of how Lake Hopatcong might supply a canal crossing New Jersey, though, as one commentator has said, "If he had been sufficiently familiar with the heights such a canal would have to surpass, he would probably have continued fishing."[1]

Coming up from the Delaware at Phillipsburg, the canal would need to rise 760 feet to pass Lake Hopatcong, so its waters could be utilized. It would then descend 914 feet to Newark, with an essentially flat addition added in 1836 taking it over to Jersey City, giving it more ready access to New York City and making it 102 miles long. Canal boats would travel in reverse from New York back to the Delaware River and often across it to Pennsylvania.

Had it been built earlier, Ben Franklin would have been unlikely to say, as he did in 1772, "Rivers are ungovernable things, especially in hilly country. Canals are quiet and very manageable."[2] One wonders what Franklin would have thought of the complex engineering of the Morris and the high hills it traversed.

Possibly more than any canal in world history, the Morris most efficiently overcame heights. It's no surprise, then, that it was often referred to as the Mountain Climbing Canal. Indeed, given all the hills it had to surmount absent any water on which mules could tow boats, it might almost be thought of as amphibious. The Morris had a total of thirty-four locks and twenty-three inclined planes. They were each numbered, with an "E" or a "W" after the number indicating how they were spaced, east and west, from Lake Hopatcong. Locks overcame short heights or descents of eight to twenty feet. Inclined planes used water-powered machinery to pull boats up or ease them down hills on rails. Three of these planes had two sets of rails so that boats heading both east and west could be raised or lowered at the same time. Lowering had to be handled with just as much care as raising. A loaded canal boat charging down an inclined plane could wreak almost unimaginable havoc on itself and its surroundings.

Plane 9W, one of those with two sets of rails, surmounted the highest of the canal's hills. It rose 100 feet, ascending rails 1,788 feet long: 1,510 to the summit and the rest to deposit the boat in the next watered section. Not far from the Delaware, the canal still has the remains of rusted rails and cables lying on its grassy hill, some of the rails still bolted to deeply buried sleeper stones. Without the inclined plane, it could have taken as many as twenty locks to get up that hill, demanding several hours and considerable labor, instead of the twelve minutes it took a boat to smoothly ascend or descend the plane on the tracks. Because of its speed and efficiency, a Morris Canal inclined plane could handle an average of thirty boats a day. During the Civil War it was commonly required to handle fifty.

The late Jim Lee lived in the plane tender's home atop the 9W hill, and in his spare time he excavated much of the inclined plane machinery— alone or with volunteers. He also produced two books on the Morris Canal, *The Morris Canal: A Photographic History* and *Tales the Boatmen Told*. There is now a small museum in the plane tender's house, which presently is owned by Warren County. Jim Lee III lives in his grandfather's house and conducts tours once a month. His father, Jim Lee Jr., has lived in the plane tender's house at 10W, even closer to the Delaware, for forty years. There is no family so associated with the Morris Canal as the Lees, who for three generations have continued their connection with and affection for it. More than anyone else, they have put the Morris Canal, even in its largely ruined state, back on the map.

Jim Lee III, his father Jim Lee Jr., and Ron Rice of the Canal Society of New Jersey (right to left) on rails still attached to the hill of inclined plane 9W, almost a hundred years since the closure of the Morris Canal.

The way an inclined plane functioned was this. In both ascending and descending, first the mules were disconnected from the canal boat where a water section ended, and the boat was floated into a huge wooden cradle car with wheels that fit the twelve-foot-wide rails. Then, water from a flat upper level was sent shooting down a pipe called a penstock onto an overshot water wheel. Later the water wheels were replaced by far more efficient Scotch turbines. The turbine was shaped like a giant pinwheel, which functioned like an enormous lawn sprinkler, the water exiting from its four nozzles and turning the turbine sixty-seven revolutions per minute. The water would then charge out of a tunnel tailrace and be conveyed to the waters of the flat canal section below.

The Morris was the very embodiment of the Industrial Revolution. With a diameter of 12.5 feet and made of cast iron, the turbine was powerful enough, as it turned, to wind or unwind a steel cable that pulled a boat, as heavy with coal as seventy tons, up or down the plane. Before steel cable was used, heavy ropes were employed and then chains, neither of which proved as adequate to the task as the cable.

When a boat ascended, reaching the next watered section, the mules again took over. Descending boats availed themselves of the same procedures

The Lees standing at and alongside sleeper stones to which rails were once attached at inclined plane 9W. On the other sleeper stones for the second rail are the rusted remains of the cable that once hauled canal boats up and down the hill.

in reverse. Those descending 9W knew they were but four miles from Port Delaware and the Delaware River. Those ascending knew they were ninety-eight miles from Jersey City.

Many boats were hinged—were in fact two boats of forty-five feet each, connected to form a vessel ninety feet in total, which could just fit in the cradle. The hinge was to ensure that the double boat could make it over the crest of the hill without being damaged.

The Morris was such an engineering marvel that interested Europeans traveled to the United States just to see and experience it. Frances Trollope, mother of the great English novelist Anthony Trollope and herself a writer of note, happened to be in the United States and immensely admired the Morris Canal in her book *Domestic Manners of the Americans* (1832). She did not like Americans and thought they were uncouth, but she did admire their engineering ability and ingenuity. Visiting the Morris just before returning to England, she wrote:

> We spent a delightful day in New Jersey in visiting . . . the inclined planes
> which are used . . . on the Morris canal. This is a very interesting work . . . which

proves the people of America to be the most enterprising in the world. . . . This canal, which connects the waters of the Hudson and the Delaware, is a hundred miles long and . . . overcomes a variation of level amounting to sixteen hundred feet. Of these, fourteen hundred are achieved by inclined planes . . . about sixty feet of perpendicular lift each. . . . There is no point in the national character of the Americans which commands so much respect as the boldness and energy with which public works are undertaken and carried out.[3]

Trollope was aware of a canal in England that used no less than twenty-nine locks and took five to six hours for a boat to ascend to a height that could have been conquered in minutes on an inclined plane.

At first complemented by railroads, then overcome by their rapidity (not to mention the development of automotive vehicles) both New Jersey canals were eventually closed to commerce, in 1924 for the Morris and 1933 for the Delaware and Raritan. At great cost, most of the Morris was obliterated, and it has been called by some since then "The Ghost Canal." The present pursuit of its details is as much an exercise in archeology and imagination as in history. For example, you might think nothing connected to the canal of a steep, paved street in Boonton, New Jersey, with the name Plane Street, but there an inclined plane once functioned. And if you were similarly oblivious while passing through a series of towns in northern New Jersey, far from any water and with no remnants of the canal, it might not strike you as strange that several of them—Port Colden and Port Murray are examples—have names with "port" as part of them. These former port cities are just as busy now as they once were on the Morris Canal. Indeed, being ports on the Morris is how, given the business the canal generated, they first came to be towns of substance.

Some of them, though, are simply historic sites. The base of plane 9W is still referred to as Port Warren, even though there is little there but a couple of houses, the foundation of what once was a store, and Lopatcong Creek, which once provided most of the water for the flat canal area just below the plane.

Some of the port towns, however, are substantial. Curious what their response would be, I have asked more than one person in these towns why they are called ports, and all I usually got in response was a shrug. "I don't know why it's called a port," one young man said. "I was born here and it's always been called Port Colden." It sounded as if he thought the town had been named at someone's whim or for no historical reason of consequence.

Why he had not been taught something about the origins of his own town's name in high school, or earlier, does not speak well for the American education system.

There is a project afoot to create the Morris Canal Greenway, a pathway across the state following the canal's route. Towns along that route, from the Delaware River on, are working with the Canal Society of New Jersey to make the greenway a reality by restoring what they can of the remnants of the canal still extant. Waterloo Village is a particularly beautiful and representative Morris Canal town, and one that has been restored. The Musconetcong River, one of the canal's key feeders, intersects with the town, which, as with plane 9W, retains the considerable remains of one of the highest inclined planes lying on a hill. It also has a canal museum, maintained by the Canal Society of New Jersey.

One day, hikers will be able to walk across the entire state on the greenway, following the canal's route. Part of that route will simply be a straight but slight depression in the woods that continues for a considerable distance, the remnant of a watered section of the canal. Even where there are few, if any, discernible remnants—strip malls and housing projects often sit where there were once sections of the canal—there are, and will be more, signs indicating the pathway of the canal. There are also sections of canal water here and there, maintained with pride by neighboring towns, but the inclined plane remnants are the true wonders of what remains of the canal.

Downriver from the Morris such a greenway (its towpath) already exists following the close to flat Delaware and Raritan Canal. Unlike the Morris, most of the D&R (which I shall henceforth call it) still flows, and alongside it is the towpath traversed by mules in the past and by hikers and bikers today. Though it was less challenging an engineering project than the Morris, since its terrain is not hilly, the D&R is equally, though perhaps not so dramatically, interesting. The fact that it required twenty-two miles of Delaware River feeder to supply sufficient water, and at a sufficient elevation to meet up with the main canal in Trenton, was certainly a remarkable feature. As its name implies, it travels from the Delaware River to the Raritan River, mostly across the narrow waist of New Jersey. Some streams enter the feeder and the main canal, augmenting their depth in drought conditions and other times entering spillways when it would otherwise be too deep.[4]

One might think of the D&R today, in its Trenton to New Brunswick main portion, as the natural divider between North and South Jersey. If New Jerseyans ever agree that there is a Central New Jersey, a gentle debate long with us, that part of the D&R will, no doubt, be considered its geographic center.

The main canal parallels the Millstone River for a considerable distance, passing over it near Princeton in a concrete aqueduct where the river enters and is the main water supply of Lake Carnegie. Near the little town of Rocky Hill, a short distance up a steep hill from the canal, is Rockingham, George Washington's last headquarters at the conclusion of the Revolutionary War. From here he would ride on horseback to Princeton's Nassau Hall where Congress was meeting. And it was also at Rockingham that Washington wrote his farewell orders to his troops and learned that the 1783 Treaty of Paris, officially ending the Revolutionary War, had been signed.

The canal continues on to such quaint and rustic villages as Griggstown, Blackwells Mills, and East Millstone, most with bridgetenders' houses, some of which are occupied, others small, informal museums or canoe rental establishments, one of which, in East Millstone, a former inn, doubles as a used book store. Swing bridges used to cross the canal at these towns, so they could be opened at the approach of canal boats which would be announced by a crew member blowing into a large conch shell horn. Today, ordinary traffic bridges cross the canal there, and only canoes, kayaks, and rowboats can pass under them.

The D&R traverses only slightly tilted land, with just a few locks (fourteen total, including those that were on the defunct Bordentown to Trenton portion) and no inclined planes. This allowed it in later years to carry motorized craft, steamboats mostly, which would have been impossible on the Morris. J. P. Morgan would occasionally travel on his huge yacht to Princeton on the canal to attend a football game.

As already discussed, the canal's main source of water is the feeder that flows to Trenton. The feeder parallels the Delaware, beginning at the hamlet of Raven Rock alongside Bull's Island and flowing through some of New Jersey's most beautiful towns, adding another element to their attractiveness. They have both the Delaware River and the canal feeder flowing alongside them, as well as the former towpath for taking a casual walk or a long hike or bike ride. Anything but motorized vehicles. One can hike or bike the whole length of the D&R, including the feeder, if one chooses, and that is true of canoeing its length as well, except for brief portages.

Bull's Island and the stream that separated it from Raven Rock was the ideal place to begin the feeder, which, like the rest of the canal, was largely dug at $1 a day by local laborers and even more cheaply by recently arrived

Irish immigrants. A considerable number (most sources say hundreds) died in a 1832–1833 Asiatic cholera epidemic, some buried in nearby cemeteries and others in unmarked, often mass, graves on the banks and on Bull's Island. A considerable number of others were buried in the Franklin Township village of Ten Mile Run (named for the stream by that name), and in Griggstown. A granite monument to their memory, first placed in New Brunswick, was mounted on Bull's Island on St. Patrick's Day in 2003—appropriate, given that the majority of those who died were Irish immigrants.

For the first several hundred feet the feeder was already half "dug," laid as it was in the stream bed alongside Bull's Island. At the northern tip of the island the water is conveyed from the Delaware into the feeder by a wing dam. One can hike to the top of Bull's Island and observe the water coming in off the Delaware. The partial dam does not hold back water so much as temporarily deepen part of the river so it is automatically conveyed into the feeder. A similar mini dam was built at Lambertville to supply the water to feed a lock that facilitated the entry of cargo boats directly into the feeder. These boats were generally smaller and lighter than those entering the main

At the northern tip of Bull's Island, where water from the Delaware is diverted into the beginnings of the D&R feeder.

The author's son Jeffrey observing Wickecheoke Creek replenishing the canal feeder. After heavy rains, its considerable excess pours into the Delaware.

canal at Bordentown. The amount of water in the feeder was augmented along its route by streams entering into it, with devices to maintain the proper water level.

The canal's main entry point for heavy cargo was Bordentown, eight miles south of Trenton, much of it coming up from Philadelphia or en route there. There was, of course, considerable commerce between New York and Philadelphia. Boats could not enter at Trenton itself because of the wall of rapids there. From Bordentown boats had to be raised by several conventional locks to reach Trenton.

Locks are sometimes familiarly referred to as "water elevators." They are used to move boats from one level to the next, either up or down. Locks have gates at both ends designed to get a boat to the level of the next area of water by temporarily either raising or lowering the water in the lock. At what is known as the Trenton Summit, both the feeder and the leg from Bordentown were united at an elevation of fifty-seven feet for the water to flow by gravity north to New Brunswick, using only occasional locks.

Thus, the D&R was originally shaped like a Y, the bottom of the letter being the leg from Bordentown to Trenton. But this eight-mile portion of the canal was abandoned when the canal was closed to commercial traffic,

The remains of the Bordentown to Trenton section of the D&R Canal, just short of its connection with the Delaware River, and the vestiges of an abandoned canal boat in the mud.

and the main canal (not including the feeder) now flows only from Trenton to New Brunswick. The section leading up from the Delaware at river's edge at Bordentown is today a muddy mess or, in the northern portion, covered by highways. The D&R is currently shaped like a V, with the feeder from Bull's Island to Trenton one side of the V and the main canal proceeding from Trenton to New Brunswick (and its entry into the Raritan River) the other side of it.

Closing the Bordentown to Trenton portion of the canal obliterated part of the inland waterway that had allowed protected travel all the way from New York to Florida, but especially between New York and Philadelphia, an important commercial and industrial corridor. Indeed, during World War II there was a strong movement to broaden and deepen the D&R, including rebuilding the Trenton to Bordentown section, so that much larger ships such as warships, could travel up and down the inland waterway, unthreatened by the Nazi U-boats lurking just offshore in the Atlantic. Closing off the Trenton-Bordentown section made it impossible for canal traffic to descend to the Delaware River at Bordentown and continue south as it had previously. Nor could it enter there after having ascended the Delaware from Philadelphia or sailing from Chesapeake Bay to Delaware Bay on the fourteen-mile canal that unites them.

The sea-level Chesapeake and Delaware Canal opened in 1829, slightly before the D&R and the Morris. Ironically, though the Army Corps of Engineers would be so emphatically criticized years later for insisting on the Tocks Island Dam, it was denounced for not moving quickly on the proposed D&R wartime expansion project. Indeed, the war ended before any work had been done on it.[5]

Making the D&R Canal especially inviting today is that the towpath once strolled by mules pulling boats behind them is still very much there and regularly maintained for recreational use. Some of the original stone mile markers still stand on the side of the towpath, not on the feeder portion but on the main canal. They contain two numbers, the distance to New Brunswick and the distance to Bordentown, always a total of forty-four miles. They were placed so that people on canal boats or leading the mules towing them could be fully aware of the distances ahead and behind them. It took a minimum of two people (one often a child) to convey a canal boat. One, often a child, kept the mules on a straight path. The second person, often the child's father, was in the boat using the rudder to keep it from being pulled into the side of the canal by the mules.

Today, it would be impossible for mules to pull a boat along the towpath from Trenton to New Brunswick. Trees line the bank between the towpath and the canal, and some are quite large. It's obvious the trees were allowed to grow once commercial traffic ended and mules no longer towed boats laden with coal. The trees would prevent a rope from being slung between a mule on the path and a boat. But now they do no harm. Their roots may even help hold the canal bank together.

While the towpath alongside the canal begins with the feeder at Bull's Island, it has been extended, alongside only the Delaware now, northward to Frenchtown and partway from Frenchtown to Milford. Twelve miles have been added to the pathway, with more to come if the train tracks all the way to Milford are removed—which is likely to happen as a Rails to Trails project because they are rarely if ever used.

Also, while the canal was originally some sixty miles long, the pathway is longer. It includes the 3.5-miles newly created from Bordentown alongside the ruin of the abandoned portion of the canal. Hopefully it can be extended so as to meet up with the towpath in Trenton, though there are obstacles in the way, including highways. Nevertheless, Delaware and

Folks walking a section of the seventy-mile D&R towpath, here along the feeder in the Lambertville area.

Raritan Canal State Park is already longer than the original canal. This linear park, passing some seventy miles through the center of New Jersey, is an environmental and recreational wonder. Indeed, given its length and availability to hikers, bikers, and canoers, it is now the second-most frequented park in New Jersey.

The D&R towpath was recently lengthened so that it could continue across Trenton without interruption, even when the canal itself is covered for one mile at the outskirts of Trenton by US Highway 1. Formerly, if you were biking or hiking, you had to make your way through the city streets of Trenton to regain access to the path—if you could find it.

But as one approaches New Brunswick, the canal and towpath end three miles earlier than they once did, because of the construction in the 1970s of an extension of Route 18 connecting the Lynch Bridge over the Raritan River on one end and downtown New Brunswick on the other. A quarter mile after Landing Lane Bridge most of the canal now empties into the Raritan and Delaware and Raritan Canal State Park ends. It is a shame that the water pouring into the Raritan blocks the path and obstructs hikers from continuing on. This would be a natural place to build a small pedestrian bridge because there is now a paved part that continues on after the torrent of water. Were this available, the towpath, including the brief paved part, would be continuous all the way from Bull's Island to Boyd Park in New Brunswick and down to the restored double entry-and-exit lock. When the canal was fully active, with boats entering and leaving the canal at the double lock, there were large seagoing ships that loaded up with the cargo of many boats and, observant of the tides, sailed on to New York. New Brunswick was a substantial port in those days.

A considerable amount of canal water is removed just before the canal pours into the Raritan. It supplies the towns and industrial areas of Central New Jersey with water. Some water is also sent through a large pipe under Route 18 and emerges three miles farther on at the beginning of Boyd Park, entering the canal, which has almost mysteriously reappeared after its three-mile hiatus, though it is admittedly quite shallow. The rustic towpath has reappeared as well, replacing the paved portion.

Thus, the D&R, except for the brief interruption of Route 18, is a linear park along the feeder and across the waist of Central New Jersey, a prime source of recreation including boating, horseback riding, biking, and hiking. Some would argue that it is more valuable today than when it carried cargo. The fact it largely flows into the Raritan establishes a connection between New Jersey's two greatest rivers, the Delaware and the Raritan. There is something wonderful about the fact that the water as one approaches New Brunswick is from a sister river on the other side of the state, a poetic intimacy one experiences with pleasure.

7

The Delaware Riviera

I hope the reader will excuse my naming my favorite New Jersey part of the Delaware River, besides the Gap, with this allusion to an elegant waterside part of France. In this chapter I'd like to discuss four New Jersey river towns I think are the prettiest ones in the state, more Vermont-like than Vermont: Lambertville, Stockton, Raven Rock, and Frenchtown, all in Hunterdon County. The towns are pretty on their own but their location on the river and towpath (and, except for Frenchtown, on the D&R feeder as well) makes them prettier. I also tend to believe that people are happier in river towns, as reflected in how such towns look and feel and the warmth with which they greet visitors. I'd like to believe that water rushing by carries away one's cares, or at least minimizes them or puts them in perspective. Perhaps it is no accident that Edward Hicks painted his famous series of "Peaceable Kingdom" paintings in the vicinity of these towns, just across the river in Bucks County, Pennsylvania.

I am not alone in harboring such sentiments about these towns and others nearby. The excellent quarterly magazine *River Towns,* focused on the Delaware's immediate surroundings, says it all in its title and the fact of its existence.

All four towns extend along Route 29, a nationally designated scenic byway. The highway is also known as the Daniel Bray Highway for reasons to be discussed in the next chapter.

Lambertville

I begin with Lambertville, the southernmost of the four towns and, I hasten to admit, my favorite. Lambertville might be considered the artistic capital of New Jersey or certainly the town with the greatest number of people in the arts, complemented by New Hope directly across the river in Pennsylvania. With the addition of New Hope's Bucks County Playhouse the area is a delightful twin city center of the arts.

The two towns have been connected by some kind of bridge from 1814 on. Lambertville has a wealth of art galleries, artist studios, antique stores, writers, filmmakers, actors, three excellent coffeehouses, terrific restaurants, lovely hotels and B&Bs—all of which says something about the town's way of life. Add to this the beauty of the D&R feeder flowing through the town—its towpath the perfect place for a peaceful walk—and the Delaware flowing just beyond it, and one has a cultivated environment complemented by a natural one. It is no accident that *Forbes* magazine chose Lambertville as one of the fifteen prettiest towns in the United States, calling it "a small town that packs a punch." The magazine went on to say that Lambertville is "a bright spot in a state that non-Jerseyans usually see through the lens of the Turnpike or the broadcasted antics and rabblerousers on its shore."[1] By "shore" I assume *Forbes* is referring to that other shore this book is decidedly *not* about. One doesn't find rabblerousers along the Delaware River. I rather think rivers, especially the Delaware, have a calming influence that brings out the best in people.

Lambertville is also on a variety of lists of the ten prettiest New Jersey towns. It was not always this way. Forty years ago, it was the town you drove through to get to New Hope, crossing the Delaware River bridge that connects them. You did that because there was little to attract one in Lambertville. Much of the town was rundown; houses were empty of residents and storefronts were boarded up. Factories were shuttered. Bats flew around inside the abandoned train station (now a magnificent restaurant, with a similarly fine inn connected to it). Indeed, Lady Bird Johnson visited Lambertville in 1965, choosing it as an example of an American town which, with some thought, could be radically improved and inaugurating there the War on Poverty and Project Head Start, which President Lyndon Johnson, made central programs of his administration.

Events in the early 1970s made the town not only dilapidated but notorious. A series of explosions from leaking gas pipes blew up four houses and killed eight people, injuring nine more. Of the two explosions on February 3, 1971, the second killed people who had evacuated houses involved in the first explosion who were now making coffee for firemen in the houses of neighbors. Not long after, yet another house blew up and killed a resident. The town became a bad joke.

Then things turned around. As has been the case elsewhere, rundown towns and neighborhoods attract artists, who generally can't afford expensive lodging and require ample studio space. The gay community also was largely responsible for the resurrection of Lambertville, as it has been of towns elsewhere in New Jersey, Asbury Park being an example. What were considered slums have been resurrected as charming nineteenth-century Victorian and Federal-style houses—especially fitting in a town where 90 percent of the buildings were built before the twentieth century. These houses and their tree-shaded streets make for an attractive and charming combination.

There is strong community spirit and friendliness in Lambertville; I always feel welcome there. In nice weather, people sit on their tiny porches chatting and greet you as you pass by. Signs decorate these porches supporting worthy causes. On a recent visit, they included the following:

KINDNESS IS EVERYTHING

WOMEN'S RIGHTS ARE HUMAN RIGHTS

BLACK LIVES MATTER

SCIENCE IS REAL

HATE HAS NO HOME HERE

FEMINISM IS FOR EVERYONE

COUNTRY BEFORE POLITICAL PARTY

NO HUMAN IS ILLEGAL

DONATIONS ACCEPTED HERE FOR WORLD'S KITCHEN

ONLY TOGETHER WILL WE END RACISM.

Also, I don't believe I've ever been in a town where the people put so much effort and imagination and fun into decorating for town events, especially Halloween, a strong example of the community spirit of the place. They do it tongue in cheek, as a goof. Literally everyone seems to decorate for Halloween, and there is even a Halloween parade. In the 1980s, before the town's rejuvenation, members of the Chamber of Commerce, aware of the Lewis Family fishery and its recent success, decided to have a two-day festival each April called the Shad Fest. Except for two years when the COVID pandemic prevented its celebration, the Shad Fest is put on each spring and attended by many thousands, everyone from town as well as many more from all parts of New Jersey and Eastern Pennsylvania, and some even coming out from New York City. One of its events is a twice daily demonstration on Lewis Island, of the crew's fishing technique, with visitors allowed onto the island to watch the fishing up close.

But still more impressive is the carnival going on in the streets of the town: the bands playing, the hundreds of vendors of interesting, often homemade objects, and the art displayed by the town's leading artists. The artists join in another way. A contest is held for a poster that will represent that year's event, and the posters are auctioned off to raise money for the community's welfare.

Lambertville, a town always eager to celebrate something.

School students also make posters of quality that are displayed. The Shad Fest is a wonderful celebration of a town and of the people who live in it.

Besides everything else in Lambertville, there is what is probably New Jersey's most interesting and varied flea market, whose full name is The Golden Nugget Antique Flea Market. It is located a bit south of the center of town on Route 29. The "Golden" part of its name derives from native son James W. Marshall, who had much to do with initiating the California Gold Rush in the 1840s. Marshall's house still stands and is the headquarters of the Lambertville Historical Society.

Stockton

> There's a small hotel
> With a wishing well
> I wish that we were there, together

The song "Small Hotel," one stanza of which is presented here, was composed by Richard Rodgers, words by Lorenz Hart, first for their Broadway musical *Jumbo* (1935) but then removed from that show and placed instead in their subsequent show, *On Your Toes* (1936). It also appeared in the movies *Words and Music* (1948), sung by Betty Garrett, and *Pal Joey* (1957), sung by Frank Sinatra. It was recorded by a host of other singers, most notably Ella Fitzgerald.

The over 300-year-old hotel on which the song is based is the Stockton Inn, in tiny Stockton, New Jersey. It was built on Main Street as a private residence in 1710, and in 1832 it was expanded into a bar and restaurant and eventually into a lovely hotel. There are historic murals inside, and the wishing well mentioned in the song is still in the patio. But as I write this, the Stockton Inn is closed and silent. First it gave up offering lodging. For years, it continued to function solely as a restaurant and bar, but recently that too faded. It has remained closed for five years, but a new owner recently purchased it, has plans to renovate it, and hopes to return it to its historic role as a magnificent hotel and eatery.

The inn was popular, particularly from the 1920s on, as a vacation resort. At that time it was owned by the Colligan family and sometimes referred to as Colligan's, sometimes as The Stockton Inn, and sometimes as Colligan's Stockton Inn. The faded name "Colligan's" can still be seen

The over 300-year-old Stockton Inn, sometimes referred to as Colligan's Stockton Inn because of the family that long owned it.

on the facade of the building. During Prohibition, the hotel was a celebrated speakeasy. The inn was favored by members of the New York intelligentsia, especially members of the Algonquin Roundtable, including Dorothy Parker, Robert Benchley, and Alexander Woollcott. Other well-known writers who stayed there included F. Scott Fitzgerald, S. J. Perelman, and Margaret Mitchell, who allegedly wrote part of *Gone With the Wind* while staying there.

Rodgers and Hart knew of the hotel partly because of its popularity among these figures plus a great number of people from the world of show business who were equally attracted to it. Band leader Paul Whiteman, who often stayed there, would end his radio and television shows with a toast to the hotel, routinely saying, wherever he was, "Goodnight. I'm going to dinner at Mrs. Colligan's." Whiteman was an important figure in his own right, but he was also the person who commissioned George Gershwin to write *Rhapsody in Blue.* The inn was the hotel of choice of stage and screen folk, many of whom vacationed there but also performed in or directed summer stock at the Bucks County Playhouse across the river. These included Helen Hayes, Clark Gable, Moss Hart (no relation to Lorenz), George S. Kaufman,

Oscar Hammerstein, Damon Runyon, and Ray Bolger. Early in life, Jacqueline Kennedy stayed there more than once.

The world at large also knew of the hotel because of the Lindbergh Baby Trial. The hotel served as a base for a number of journalists covering the trial of Bruno Hauptmann for allegedly kidnapping and murdering the child of the famed aviator. The trial was taking place some twenty miles away in the 1828 courthouse of Flemington, the Hunterdon County seat, but hotel space there was limited. In what was often referred to as "The Trial of the Century," there were times when the packed old courthouse was surrounded by thousands of people awaiting revelations and finally the verdict, which attracted even more attention.

The owner of the Stockton Inn was to say, "In 1935 during the Hauptmann trial . . . reporters . . . lived here. They set up a newsroom and based all their operations here. That's when people really noticed us." The combination of the journalists covering the Hauptmann trial, the celebrities who favored it, and the Rodgers and Hart musical, all happening almost simultaneously, made the Stockton Inn one of the most famous hotels in the country and more than anything put Stockton, New Jersey, and the river and canal feeder that flowed yards away, on the map.

With the hotel closed, Stockton is today noteworthy for other reasons. On the outskirts of town, a short way north on Route 29, are some ancient buildings on the bank of the canal feeder called the Prallsville Mills, a favorite of landscape painters. Built in 1720, it is one of the great features of the Delaware and Raritan Canal State Park. While owned by New Jersey, the Delaware River Mill Society manages the property under a long-term lease with the state. This was necessary because the state had no funds for preserving the mills and had almost sold the site to a developer who planned to build a strip mall there. The society's members are dedicated to preserving the mills, interpreting their history, and making them available to its members and the public at large for cultural, social, and community activities. Once featuring saw, grist, and linseed oil mills, powered by the Wickecheoke Creek that runs beside it, the mills still have much of their machinery intact. But rather than being in the way, it adds charm and history to what is a lovely social center, art gallery, concert hall, and much sought-after wedding site, not to mention that instead of becoming a strip mall, it is on the National Register of Historic Places.

The Prallsville Mills on the outskirts of Stockton.

Raven Rock

Raven Rock is today a tiny unincorporated hamlet midway between Stockton and Frenchtown. It is so small one might drive by without noticing it, and it doesn't always appear on New Jersey maps. A stone monolith one hundred feet high towers over it. Since many of its few houses are made of stone, from a distance they appear to be built into the mountain like an abandoned Indian village out West. One is uncertain whether to think of the mountain as protecting the houses below or in imminent danger of crushing them. I asked residents why this spot was chosen for settlement in the eighteenth century. One said, "The rock cuts down on the wind." Another opined, "Backed up against the mountain the settlement couldn't be attacked by Indians from the rear."

A clear disadvantage of the town's location is that rainwater runs down the mountain and must be diverted around the houses. And when there is a major storm and the Delaware overflows its banks, it sometimes reaches these houses, as the river's floodplain extends to the mountain.

The village fronts on both the canal feeder and the river itself. Indeed, it is at Raven Rock that the canal feeder begins the sixty-mile voyage of the Delaware and Raritan Canal. Just off Raven Rock is Bull's Island, from

Typical of the architecture in Raven Rock is the abandoned stone Saxtonville Tavern. One can see the beginning of the giant rock behind it, its lower parts forested.

whose northern tip one may discern a partial, almost indiscernible wing dam or weir that temporarily deepens the Delaware so as to convey water into the beginnings of the feeder, which was originally a creek that flowed between the island and the town.

In its heyday, when the canal flourished, 150 people lived in Raven Rock and on Bull's Island, which today is part of the D&R Canal State Park. The settlement had its own post office, grocery store, blacksmith shop, basket factory, mill, fishery, and tavern. It has none of these things today but has not lost any of its charm. The beautiful stone Saxtonville Tavern, built in 1782 and now abandoned, would make a splendid hotel or restaurant, if restored. Nathaniel Saxton was such a prominent citizen that the town's name was briefly changed to Saxtonville, later returning to its original, more poetic name of Raven Rock.

As the D&R Canal feeder was being dug, the town further prospered by offering services and provisions to canal workers and later to those manning the boats that came over from Pennsylvania. The canal feeder was more than a supplier of water to the canal at this point. It made Raven Rock something of a lively little port. Smaller, less weighty boats could enter the feeder at Raven Rock, somewhat larger ones through a lock at Lambertville where the feeder, because of tributaries entering it, especially the one at Prallsville, was more ample.

Now, only fifteen people live in Raven Rock. For some fifteen more it is a weekend or vacation retreat. The scanty population is often augmented by landscape painters, for whom Raven Rock is a favorite subject. Where one may often see a number of people—bikers, hikers, and roller skaters—is on the pedestrian bridge crossing the canal, the island, and the Delaware en route to equally tiny Lumberville in Pennsylvania.

Characteristic of those one meets in the hamlet or on the bridge is their uncertainty as to the origin of the name Raven Rock. A painter told me it is a translation of the Lenape word *Mauanissing*. A bicyclist said, "It must be because the rock is black—only it isn't, so it must be the ravens circling the rock." I looked up several times with my binoculars, and there were birds, but clearly hawks, not ravens. Still another painter, pointing to the fissure in the rock that runs down the middle of it, suggested that "raven" is a modern pronunciation of "riven."

There are two roads in Raven Rock. Route 29, of course, but also the unpaved Quarry Road, which ascends alongside the rock monolith. Past the quarry, where uranium was found (too little, as it turned out, to be mined), the road flattens, eventually leading to the nearly 300-year-old Rosemont Cemetery, the names in its oldest section reflecting Raven Rock's history. Principal among them is Daniel Bray, whose essential contributions to George Washington's efforts on the Delaware during the Revolutionary War will be discussed in the next chapter.

Frenchtown

I said earlier that among the wonderful New Jersey towns along the river, Lambertville is the finest. But Frenchtown, though smaller, is equally charming. Like Lambertville, it appears on the list of New Jersey's ten most beautiful towns. Its downtown area is also on the National Register of Historic Districts.

One thing that has made Frenchtown more interesting in recent years is the extension of the towpath to and beyond it in the direction of Milford. To be clear, the D&R feeder does not extend beyond Bull's Island and Raven Rock, just the towpath does, along which nothing was ever towed along this section of it. The removal of old train tracks made this possible. Extending the towpath made the Delaware and Raritan State Park larger and connected Frenchtown on foot or by bike with the other lovely towns just south of it and on from there to Trenton and across New Jersey, following the Delaware and Raritan Canal. Additional train tracks north of Frenchtown may yet be removed, extending the path and park as far as Milford.

Frenchtown has Art Yard, a wonderful facility for exhibiting internationally and regionally renowned artists. Included are monumental sculptures that are part of its permanent collection, at the Yard but also in various places around town. It has a residency program and has bought up housing around town for its residents. Art Yard also has a large new performance space for music, dance, and theatre with 162 seats. Each row of seats is considerably elevated over the one in front, of it, so everyone in the audience can see well without any strain. I was told that the Baryshnikov Arts Center in New York City partners with Art Yard, and that the great dancer and choreographer Mikhail Baryshnikov has looked over the performance space at Art Yard and pronounced it outstanding, especially because "from any seat, you can see each performer's feet, essential to dance performance."

Frenchtown has other advantages. Every store is interesting (there is even one specializing in the occult), and there is a great variety of restaurants. Hardly a place in town isn't attractive.

Most important, it has a bookstore, with regular presentations by authors and even musicians. Bookstores are increasingly and sadly a rarity in the age of Amazon and especially so in small towns. But the Frenchtown bookstore carries on nevertheless, with a great variety of book presentations and signings by writers and mini-concerts by musicians. Bookstores are a sign of civilization. Would that every town had one.

Frenchtown has a remarkable history of attracting writers of the first rank. James Agee rented a house for a year in the 1930s next to what is now City Hall, while writing *Let Us Now Praise Famous Men*. Elizabeth Gilbert, author of *Eat, Pray, Love*, lived in Frenchtown for several years while she and her then husband ran an Asian art import business in what later became Art Yard before it built more elaborate facilities nearby, the older building continuing to figure in its ambitious agenda. Nathaniel West stayed for a while in the Frenchtown Inn (built in 1805) and is believed to have completed his masterpiece, *Miss Lonelyhearts*, during that period.

In mentioning the Frenchtown Inn, I am reminded that the town has another hotel a couple of blocks away, the National, where residents have tended to live for extended periods of time rather than tourists or visitors.

Every corner in Frenchtown is charming.

Ben Coombs was such a person. Such was his dedication to Frenchtown and this hotel that his last wish was to have his cremains placed in a bottle on a shelf in the bar behind bottles of liquor. And there they are to this day. Only in Frenchtown!

Frenchtown has a light, fun-loving touch, a sense of humor about itself. Even calling itself Frenchtown has a non-serious side. Its first settler was Paul Henri Mallet-Prevost, who did speak French but was of Swiss origin. Nevertheless, on July 14, Bastille Day, the town turns itself inside out in a wonderful celebration of its "French roots," something like Lambertville's Shad Fest. For one day Frenchtown is French and especially charming.

Frenchtown's humor and light spirit is, for me, represented by the large tombstone that stands half hidden in the woods in what is the backyard of a house on Tremont Street. It is just off the crushed rock path a bit south of the center of town, the part added to the Delaware and Raritan Canal State Park. I must have passed it five times on different walks before I spotted it.

Jonathan R. Kugler (1824–1891) and Anna Kugler (1827–1910) are memorialized on it. But what is their tombstone doing there? I asked the librarian at the Frenchtown library. She told me that she had lived in Frenchtown her whole life and never seen the tombstone. However, she put me in touch with the gentleman who has served for many years as superintendent of the

Frenchtown cemetery, just a hundred yards up the hill facing the front of the house. We met there and he showed me a more modern tombstone with the exact same details. "I think they're buried here," he said, "but the stone is 1940s style."

"So, who's buried under the other stone?" I asked.

"I don't know," he said. "Maybe nobody. I have the feeling that when these people died nobody paid the stone carver and, so, he threw the stone out when he retired. Later, other family members, without knowing of the older stone, paid for a new one and had it set up in the cemetery. But that's just what I suppose."

I went and inquired of the folks who owned the house. They told me that their barn had indeed once been the shop of a memorial carver and that, buying their house, the first thing they did was clean up the unfathomable amount of debris just outside the barn, mostly branches and other brush. "It was about twenty feet deep," the woman said. "At the bottom of it all we found the stone, three sections detached but intact, the fourth, a decorative element on top, broken."

"We set up the stone where it now stands," the man said.

"Why?" I asked.

"I get a kick out of watching people on the trail. Most of them don't spot it. Those that do stop, scratch their heads, and wonder why two people from long ago seem to be buried in the woods in our backyard."

"Anything in particular about the people who stop?" I asked.

"No," he replied, laughing. "Just people like you."

Now I was the one laughing. I wouldn't know how to explain it, but it seems to me that this story is typical of Frenchtown. People just don't take things too seriously there. There is a lightness of spirit. Maybe that's why I like to go there with a friend fairly often, have lunch, and just hang out or walk the towpath.

I always enjoy myself in Frenchtown.

I enjoy myself in all four of these towns on the Jersey Riviera. They're the perfect response to those who stereotype New Jersey as second rate or mediocre, the whole state an extension of the Turnpike. The stereotype of New Jersey is largely a New York (or rather a midtown Manhattan) product. Those living in what is often referred to as the Outer Boroughs often catch similar grief. Some of the putdown of New Jersey, I would wager, emanates from jealousy.

8

Washington's Crossing(s)

The reader will recall that in the first chapter I mentioned that the Delaware is a waterway soaked in history, far more so than the towns and beaches of New Jersey on the Atlantic. The reader will also notice that this chapter is not titled "Washington's Crossing" but "Washington's Crossing(s)," for four crossings of the Delaware were made by Washington and his troops within a short period of time in December 1776, not just the one every American is familiar with. Despite its splendid tribute to George Washington and his brave revolutionary army, I sometimes wonder whether the annual Christmastime reenactment of Washington's crossing, with thousands of spectators on both the New Jersey and Pennsylvania banks, tends to perpetuate the myth of a single crossing of the Delaware.

I do not mean to limit the significance of Washington's crossing of the icy Delaware in freezing weather with his army on the night of December 25–26, 1776, and, after marching nine miles to Trenton, handily vanquishing the Hessian mercenaries there, with few casualties on both sides. Incidentally, should the reader wish to take a nice hike that reenacts history, Washington's route to Trenton, part of which is referred to as "Continental Lane," is fairly well marked with signs and can be followed from his New Jersey landing site right down to the Hessian barracks.

The Battle of Trenton would prove to be the first victory of significance for the Americans in the Revolutionary War and provide some confidence that our striving for independence was not a hopeless venture. But in addition to the annual reenactments, the crossing and its aftermath is almost exclusively associated in American minds with Emanuel Gottlieb Leutze's *Washington Crossing the Delaware* (1851), probably America's most famous historical painting. I might mention that while the huge painting is the property of and currently hangs in the Metropolitan Museum of Art in New York, it was on loan to Washington Crossing State Park in Pennsylvania for ten years. Also, Leutze painted a smaller version of it that was recently sold at auction for $45 million. Another version, probably the first, was damaged in a fire in Leutze's studio, restored, and later destroyed in the Kunsthalle Bremen art museum in Germany by Allied bombs at the close of World War II. Further, other artists have painted copies of it almost indistinguishable from Leutze's or have painted parodies of it.

Emanuel Leutze was of German origin but spent his formative years in Philadelphia, where his family had fled to escape perpetual wars and persecution in Germany. He went back to Germany to study painting in Düsseldorf but returned to America for an extended period of time later in life, his

Emanuel Leutze's 1851 painting *Washington Crossing the Delaware*. Courtesy of the Metropolitan Museum of Art in New York City.

likely second version of *Washington Crossing the Delaware* brought with him. In a sense, then, he was both German and American. One side of him regarded his painting celebrating American liberty as an inspiration for what he hoped would be democracy in Germany. The painting also proved something of an inspiration to other European countries struggling with attempts at unity and freedom. But it was in America that it was a sensation, exhibited in New York and in Washington, with thousands lined up to see it.

In America it produced considerable pride, and Leutze became something of an American hero. Many a household had a print, engraving, or needlework displayed on its wall or mantel. It can be safely said that it is first not only among American historic paintings but patriotic ones as well.

But the very freedom and unity Leutze celebrated in America was soon to be a disappointment to him, to say the least. He was in the United States during the Civil War, which he regarded as the destruction of everything he held dear. Like many well-meaning people, including Abraham Lincoln, the abolition of slavery was not his principal concern; preserving the Union was. Before the war he was commissioned by Congress to paint another enormous historic painting, *Westward the Course of Empire Takes Its Way*, which hangs in the Capitol to this day. When Leutze died in 1868, he was buried in Washington, completing the circle of his dual nationality.

There is much more to the story, as well as aspects of this painting that are misleading or simply inventions. First, the father of our country, however heroic in appearance, did not cross the Delaware in a crowded rowboat, much less standing and with what appears to be one foot either on a seat or on the gunwale near the bow, the perfect position to turn the boat over in the icy water, if nothing else did first. He was actually aboard a Durham boat, the workhorses of the Delaware, usually employed to transport some fifteen tons of heavy cargo such as pig iron or coal or used as ferries. Given their nature, it is easy to see how they could carry the heavy equipment Washington needed to transport. They are believed to be the creation of Robert Durham, for whom the town of Durham, Pennsylvania is named, and early in the eighteenth century some one hundred of them plied the waters of the Delaware. They were flat-bottomed, came to a point on both ends, and were usually forty to sixty feet long and six to eight feet wide. They were as heavy and steady as wooden boats could be. Washington was crossing the icy river with 2,400 men but, equally important, with a cargo of horses and cannon. Rowboats would never have served.[1] The Durham boat has often been referred to as "The Boat That Won the Revolutionary War."[2]

Given that Washington is known to have had only fourteen Durham boats and a couple of smaller ones, his army almost certainly must have crossed the Delaware in shifts, which is part of what delayed their arrival in Trenton. Indeed, some historians believe it took the army ten hours for everyone to cross, so that they were not fully assembled on the New Jersey banks until 4 A.M. They had planned to attack during the night but could not do so until after daylight, at 8:00 in the morning, it taking four hours to march nine miles through the snow and sleet to get to Trenton.

There is much else that is invented in Leutze's painting. The stars-and-stripes flag aboard the boat was not designed and chosen by the Continental Congress until six months after the crossing. It is generally believed that if there was a flag aboard Washington's boat it was the blue one with a sprinkling of stars, customary until then. The flag in the painting is held by James Monroe, then an officer in the army, who was not aboard Washington's boat but had gone on earlier with fifty men to scout the terrain between where Washington would land and Trenton. Monroe was seriously wounded in the battle. Had he not survived, American history would be absent a certain two-term president (1817–1825) and proponent of the Missouri Compromise and Monroe Doctrine.

Also, there appears to be a Black man, an Indigenous American, and a woman among the rowers; the woman is virtually never mentioned by historians discussing this painting. The Black man is believed by some historians to be based on Prince, a slave of General William Whipple of the New Hampshire militia. He is close to Washington's right hand. The Native American is at the back of the boat (identified by his clothes and the beaded bag he carries). The woman is two-thirds of the way back, on the right side, in a red coat and a frilly scarf, with a woman's diminutive facial features, small hands, and an attractive bracelet. She is also the only one on the boat without a hat so it is much easier to see, with her extensive hair and its style, that she is distinctly female. Much as the presence of these people aboard Leutze's crafted boat might be seen as a celebration of American diversity and idealism—combatting racism, prejudice toward Indigenous peoples, and sexism—none of these people are believed to have been aboard Washington's boat. A much more accurate portrayal of the boat and its occupants may be found on a relief by Thomas Eakins on the Battle Monument in Trenton.

As I write this there is a special show at the Metropolitan Museum in New York of Leutze's painting accompanied by what seems to be a satire of it by the distinguished African American artist Robert Colescott titled *George Washington Carver Crossing the Delaware: Page from an American History Textbook* (1975). Everyone aboard the boat is Black, including the eminent agricultural scientist George Washington Carver, who stands in George Washington's position. Not only that: many of the boat's occupants are caricatures based on how Black people were seen and depicted, and in some quarters are still, by a racist society. At the back of the boat is someone not rowing but playing the banjo while smoking a cigar, and up front is a crewmember dressed as a chef with a billowing white hat. I'm glad that Colescott joins me in seeing a woman in the boat, but he has painted her as very much overweight, somewhat suggestive of the traditional Black Mammy. Whether his intention is to underscore Black contributions to American history, to parody Leutze's painting, or to portray ugly Black stereotypes in a comic fashion to point them out is not entirely clear. Perhaps it is a little of all three.

Nevertheless, there were Massachusetts and Rhode Island regiments in the Continental Army that were integrated with Black (slave and free) and Native American fighters who were instrumental to Washington's success in Trenton and elsewhere. This was even more significant because the British were offering freedom to any Black slave who would fight on their side. Ironically and shamefully, the Continental Army was more integrated at that time than it would be again until after World War II, when President Harry Truman ended the segregation of America's armed forces with the stroke of a pen. Indeed, Congress recently passed a bill to erect a memorial on or near the National Mall to honor Black and Indigenous soldiers of the Revolutionary War. But one can still take pleasure in Colescott's and Leutze's celebration of American aspirations, however different and, in each case, divorced from reality.

Leutze's painting is often parodied or used to make fun of contemporary America. A cover of the *New Yorker* magazine had a cartoon by Barry Blitt of Washington's boat titled *Crossing the Divide*, with everyone aboard hitting each other with their oars, and one crew member biting Washington's leg. Part of the crew and Washington insist on heading in one direction, the other half in another, a reference to the great divide in current American life and how it may contrast with the patriotism and relative unity inherent in the nation's origins—at least as we may choose to see them, as does Leutze.[3]

It must be mentioned that the crossing of the Delaware that is routinely celebrated was Washington's second. After all, he had to cross the Delaware to get to Pennsylvania, from where he would launch the crossing depicted in Leutze's painting and in reenactments each year. This first crossing was on December 4, 1776. It was the final act of the army's flight across New Jersey just ahead of a superior British force. The British had taken over Manhattan, including the fort in what we now call Washington Heights. With the bulk of the army, Washington crossed the Hudson to New Jersey and, at Fort Lee, watched the British finish off his fort in New York. Knowing they would soon cross in pursuit of him, his army moved as quickly as it could across New Jersey toward the Delaware.

Reaching the Raritan River, much of Washington's army crossed the wooden covered bridge where Landing Lane Bridge is today. Then they destroyed the bridge so the British could not avail themselves of it. With the British close behind them, other parts of the army crossed the Raritan a few miles downstream. They were supported by a battery of cannon and commanded by Alexander Hamilton, who fired over them at the British from the hill where stands Old Queens, the venerable building which once was the only university building and today houses the offices of the Rutgers University president and top university staff.

Knowing that even if he could safely cross all of New Jersey he would then be backed up against the Delaware, the ever-resourceful Washington had commissioned Captain Daniel Bray to precede the army to the Delaware and gather as many boats as possible, especially Durhams, so that they would be on hand when the army arrived. Bray was a wise choice because he had grown up along the Delaware and knew the river and its people intimately, especially in the area discussed in the previous chapter, which is not very far from where Washington crossed.

Bray was able to convince neighbors to loan their Durham boats; when they would not, he simply absconded with them, often having to cut them out of the ice. In 1903, the poet Joseph Folsom wrote "The Ballad of Daniel Bray," which appears in various collections of patriotic American poetry. A large portion of New Jersey's Route 29, which through what I've called "The Delaware Riviera," is today called The Daniel Bray Highway.

Arriving at the Delaware, Washington and his army began boarding the boats Bray had collected. After everyone arrived in Pennsylvania, the boats were hidden behind a heavily wooded island that was close to the shore so that they could not be seen by the British army, which soon arrived on the Jersey shore. With no boats to cross (Bray had destroyed the ones unsuitable to Washington's purposes), the British settled down for what they assumed would be the rest of the winter in an encampment near the river.

The Christmastime crossing was south of where the British Army was camped and was completed at night to avoid detection. The attack on the Hessians in Trenton was an unqualified success, including the capture of 918 Hessians and abundant military stores, including many muskets and several cannon. A rumor that must be dispelled (it is in many history books) is that Washington's troops won this battle because the Hessians were drunk from Christmas celebrations. This appears to be untrue. Washington won the battle handily, partly because the fierce wind, sleet, and snow were at his troops' backs and in the faces of the Hessians, who could hardly see and, because of the wet weather, and being ill-prepared, found many of their muskets misfiring. After a short battle they surrendered.

In order that the Hessians not again be a force to contend with, Washington marched them along with his army the nine miles back to the boats and crossed back to the Pennsylvania side, with undoubtedly even more trips than those preceding the Battle of Trenton and with considerable anxiety as to when the British Army would arrive at the Delaware. This constituted the third crossing of the Delaware. The Hessian mercenaries were initially kept as prisoners in Newtown, Pennsylvania. After the war, some of them settled in the United States and became American citizens.

Washington spread out his troops along the bank to preclude a British attack that would not only have menaced his army but opened the way for the British to march on Philadelphia. But an attack continued to be unlikely because the British had no boats. They considered and then rejected building them. They also hoped the Delaware would entirely freeze over so that they might attack by charging across the river, but the Delaware, though full of chunks of ice, was unlikely to freeze over, as is the case with most swiftly flowing rivers.

Totally outsmarted by Washington, the British could hardly imagine that he would cross the Delaware *again*. But on the night of December 29–30, Washington crossed a fourth time, this time directly to Trenton, taking over the town. The British, under General Cornwallis, were infuriated and went on the attack on January 2, 1777. But Washington was now reinforced by units of his army that had not been present during the battle with the Hessians. He had also placed his cannons on a hill overlooking the town. Retreating across a bridge to the south side of

Assunpink Creek, which flows into the Delaware, Washington fired each time the British attempted to cross that bridge. This is known as the Second Battle of Trenton, a term some historians accept and others feel is not fitting because, they argue, the fight was not sufficiently substantial an altercation to be thought of as a "battle" or even much worthy of discussion. My own view is that it was battle enough and that such folks are laboring under the misapprehension that only Washington's crossing leading to the attack on the Hessians is worthy of notice, once again helping to perpetuate the myth of the single crossing of December 25–26.

When darkness fell on January 2, the British, who greatly outnumbered the Americans, camped on one side of the Assunpink, determined to launch a major attack the morning of the next day, January 3. But Washington had huge bonfires lit and, in the middle of the night, muffling the wheels of his cannon and leaving a few troops behind to keep the fires blazing, he and his army escaped in the direction of Princeton, where there was a smaller British contingent headquartered in Princeton University's Nassau Hall and where the American Congress would meet at the conclusion of the war. There is, to this day, the mark of an American-fired cannon ball in the stone wall of the south side of Nassau Hall.

When the British camped on the Assunpink awakened the morning of January 3, they were shocked to discover that the American army was no longer on the other side of the creek. They immediately headed for Princeton but were hours late, arriving after the Americans had triumphed in the Battle of Princeton and departed. Thus, given Washington's continuing military genius, America would have its hopes supported, during what has come to be known as the "Ten Crucial Days" (December 25–January 3), that victory and independence from Britain was possible. These victories also served to immensely aid recruitment, something that had persistently preoccupied Washington before then.[4]

The Americans headed from Princeton to Morristown where, beginning on January 6, they would spend the rest of the winter of 1776–1777. They were back again for the exceptionally cold winter of 1779–1780. One thing no New Jerseyan can understand is why so much is made of the winter of 1777–1778 at Valley Forge, Pennsylvania, while so little is said about the two winters spent in Morristown under equally difficult circumstances. Valley Forge is a major tourist attraction, while little attention is paid to Morristown's importance in the Revolutionary War, even among people who live in Morristown. The Pennsylvanians seem to be more clever than New Jerseyans at awakening interest in and celebrating their state's history.

Having visited Washington's Crossing, Pennsylvania, and Washington's Crossing, New Jersey, one may perceive a similar disparity. Washington's Crossing, Pennsylvania, is immediately there when one crosses the bridge, and there is even the village of Washington's Crossing in addition to the campground and museum. Admittedly, George Washington was in Pennsylvania for the better part of a month before the first Trenton attack and returned there after it, whereas Washington's Crossing, New Jersey, is just where the army, having crossed the river, began its march to Trenton and to which it returned with its Hessian prisoners. Still, it is a bit difficult to locate the museum at Washington's Crossing, New Jersey. It is in the hills above the river, and the signage directing you there is scant. On one day there I found myself the only visitor, and this was a weekend day. The Pennsylvania side had an abundance of people even though New Jersey has a finer museum. Is this an example of New Jersey's inferiority complex vis-à-vis Philadelphia and especially New York City, an example of its lackluster attempt to sell itself and Pennsylvania's ability to do so more ably?

Or should New Jersey be celebrated for its greater modesty? I'll leave it to readers to decide.

9

Napoleon's Brother
on the Banks of the
Delaware

Hiking through the woods outside Bordentown, New Jersey, on a high bluff, you get an occasional glimpse of Crosswicks Creek far below, just at the point where it enters the Delaware. George Washington sank some boats in Crosswicks to keep the British from getting them—then resurrected them when that danger was past. The woods seem like any other woods until you come across a stone staircase descending a hill some thirty to forty feet. It is perfectly steady; you can walk up and down it. What is an elegant stone staircase doing in the middle of the woods? Surely, it once sat inside a house but, if so, where is the house or any sign of it? If you continue on through the woods, you might next come across a tunnel in the hillside. No one knows if it was for deliveries to a house or for its occupants to escape when threatened or both. If you keep going you encounter a deteriorating small brick bridge spanning a gully, probably once part of a carriage road. These woods are haunted by the past.

The trees have obviously appeared and grown since Joseph Bonaparte lived here for most of the period between 1817 and 1839, occasionally returning to Europe for short visits—to England rather than to his native France,

Steps in the forest, probably from Joseph Bonaparte's second house.

A tunnel, possibly leading both to and from Joseph Bonaparte's second house. Was it for deliveries, escape, or both?

The remains of a bridge in the forest, likely part of the miles of elaborate carriage roads Joseph Bonaparte favored for his guests to enjoy.

where he would likely have found himself endangered in that post-Napoleon time. What was he doing on this New Jersey hillside alongside the Delaware River? We shall discuss this but, for the moment, I should say that his story, as with Washington's four crossings, is another example of the history that pervades the banks of the Delaware.

Joseph was Napoleon's older brother. He didn't share his brother's militaristic ambitions and had little to do with Napoleon's aim to be emperor not only of France but all of Europe, if not most of the world. Joseph enjoyed the good life and was more of a playboy, though he was also a patron of the arts and well read. Absent any keen enthusiasm, he acceded to Napoleon's wishes that he serve as King of Naples (1806–1808), which included virtually all of Italy south of Naples including Sicily. Then his brother moved him to a more important crown, that of Spain. Even before Napoleon was defeated the first time and exiled to the Isle of Elba in 1814, Joseph felt himself to be no longer safe in Spain. The Spanish people were increasingly in revolt against the rule of a foreigner and, even though Joseph was king, the French generals who dominated Spain militarily took their orders from Napoleon. Joseph was essentially a figurehead.

Still, one must remember how the French dominated, mistreated, and butchered the Spaniards during his reign. While the great painter Francisco Goya was initially attracted to some of Napoleon's liberalizing ideas, he turned against the French when he witnessed Spaniards dying of starvation in the streets of Madrid or slaughtered there. French barbarism was the subject of Goya's great painting *The Third of May, 1808*, which shows the execution of Spanish patriots, and of the eighty-two etchings called *The Disasters of War*. These works essentially document the period when Joseph Bonaparte was king and were an indictment of what Goya now saw as Spain's murderous French rulers. It is interesting to pass through the Plaza de Independencia in Madrid, which celebrates the successful effort to rid Spain of French domination. This, of course, included getting rid of Joseph and reinstalling a Spanish king, Fernando VII, on the throne. The Spanish War of Independence, also called the Peninsular War, has as its dates the years 1808–1814, the very years Joseph sat on Spain's throne.

Sentiments similar to those of the Spaniards echoed throughout most of Europe. For example, the origin of the mafia in Sicily (the word "mafia" means "refuge") was a band of guerilla patriots fighting against French domination. Only later did the mafia become identified with crime.

I have often wondered how it is that Napoleon is regarded by most Frenchmen as a, if not *the*, national hero. He had some good ideas—his Napoleonic Code supported women's rights (though he later reversed himself), fought to end feudalism, advocated public education, and knocked down the walls of ghettos barring Jews from full citizenship—but, in the main, he could be seen as a vainglorious tyrant and, in effect, a mass murderer. It is interesting that Hitler seemed to proceed geographically in a manner almost identical to Napoleon's, conquering virtually all of Europe and North Africa and then advancing on to the vast lands of Russia, where long supply lines heralded the beginning of the end for both of them. When the Nazis subjugated Paris in 1940, and Hitler went there to relish his triumph, one of the first things he did was visit Napoleon's tomb.

I have also wondered why several books by Americans on Joseph consider him "the gentle Bonaparte." He may have been gentler than his imperialistic brother, with no desire to conquer the world, or certainly not to fight in wars, but when I mentioned his alleged kindness to Spanish historian friends, they laughed at what they considered my naivete. "That's the trouble with you Americans," one said indignantly. "Because you've never had a king or royal family, you lust after them." Indeed, the then governor of New Jersey, Mahlon Dickerson, wrote to Joseph: "I take this opportunity of expressing to you the sincere gratification I feel at the partiality you have shown this State by selecting it as the place of your residence." Like the governor, New Jerseyans, especially people from Bordentown, tended to fawn over Joseph Bonaparte, as if by living among them he brought them honor and prestige.[1] Folks from Bordentown with whom I have spoken seem to still feel this way.

Another of my Spanish friends told me, "Because Americans know nothing of Joseph Bonaparte's activities in Spain, you celebrate his decision to live in your country. We know better." I believe I can safely assume what my Spanish friends in general would think of a book titled *The Gentle Bonaparte: A Biography of Joseph, Napoleon's Elder Brother*, which celebrates "not the Great Bonaparte, before whom all bowed but few loved, but the gentle Bonaparte, who was loved by all."[2]

Joseph fled Spain in 1814 and is widely believed to have taken the crown jewels and other things of immense value, including some of Spain's finest paintings. In short, he came to America with great, otherwise unexplainable wealth. He had already shipped fifty Spanish paintings out of the country but, as he tried to leave with more, was stopped by the British, who relieved him of the paintings he had with him. He was lucky they didn't look in his baggage, which likely contained his most important riches. The British were in league with the Spaniards against the French, as were the Portuguese. Joseph was not independently wealthy yet would live on the Delaware as if he were still a king, almost certainly because of the valuable things he stole from Spain and sold at extraordinary prices. He purchased vast lands in Upper New York State that he occasionally visited and purchased chateaux in both France and Switzerland in which, in his absence, members of his family lived.

When he first came to America in 1815 he lived briefly in New York and then in Philadelphia under the assumed name of the Comte (Count) de Survilliers, a title he apparently maintained until he learned that he was not in danger in his adopted country and could safely resume use of his real name and former title, profiting by all that came with it.

Wishing to return to his luxurious life as a former king, he bought extensive New Jersey lands overlooking the Delaware in an area known as Point Breeze, outside the center of Bordentown, that eventually amounted to some 1,800 beautifully landscaped acres. His formal gardens fascinated his neighbors and visitors—representing a different approach than America's tendency to evoke the natural in its gardens. Adding to the "cultured" aspect of his gardens were many statues of classical figures. Some visitors were shocked to see such nudity, but most attributed it to European sophistication. He also kept swans and other ornamental birds on a lake he created down by the river. He built no less than twelve miles of carriage roads and delighted in taking his visitors for rides about his estate. People in Bordentown took great pride that a former king was living on a hill on the outskirts of town and universally hoped for invitations to be received there.

Inside the house was a large wine cellar. Joseph's nickname, given to him by Spaniards, had been *Pepe Botellas* ("Joe Bottles"), because of his prodigious consumption of alcohol. The house also featured floor-to-ceiling mirrors, marble fireplaces, and grand staircases, as well as one of the greatest collection of paintings in the world and a library of over 8,000 volumes, larger than that of Thomas Jefferson, whose collection was the foundation of the Library of Congress. Joseph loved poetry and was a student of ideas—so much so that he was invited to membership in the American Academy of the Arts and Sciences and the American Philosophical Society, the latter founded by Ben Franklin. No one questioned his less-than-salutary political background. Both societies admitted him with pleasure and treated him as a celebrity.

His 40,000-square-foot palatial house's only rival in the United States was the White House. For a period in its history, Bordentown had the nickname "The King's City." When his palace caught fire, Joseph was away for the day, so it is testimony to the high regard citizens of Bordentown had for him, or the pleasure they took in having a royal as a neighbor, that many rushed to the site and removed whatever they could of value before the palace was entirely consumed.

Though the burning of his first mansion was considered an accident, rumor had it that a local woman, an immigrant from Russia and a servant at the estate, set the fire to avenge Napoleon's invasion of her country. Those

An 1832 watercolor on paper of Joseph Bonaparte's second home, by Karl Bodmer. Reproduction and permission to use the painting in this book is provided by the Joslyn Museum in Omaha, Nebraska, where the original resides along with a collection of other Bodmer works. The Historical Society of Bordentown assisted in my efforts to obtain a copy of the painting.

artifacts I encountered in the woods were probably the remnants of his second house, since the first house was less high up and closer to the rivers. Eventually, the second mansion was torn down by a British diplomat who built a Victorian mansion close to its site, which also was eventually torn down, making identifying to which of the three houses artifacts belonged a challenge for archeologists, though the site of the first house, closer to the river, has recently been excavated.[3]

Joseph had come to America without his wife Julie and their two daughters. He was not to see his wife again for twenty-five years, something none of his American biographers seem to question. Both daughters would briefly live with him in his castle-like home, the older one with her husband, but mostly in a smaller house he had built for them down by the rivers alongside the small artificial lake he created by damming Thornton Creek, which ran on his property. The lake was for many years a popular ice-skating site for the people of Bordentown. Indeed, an oil on canvas mural titled *Skating on Bonaparte's Pond*, painted by Avery F. Johnson in 1940, hangs in the Bordentown Post Office.

Elements of the more modest house built for his daughter and her husband still mark the spot where it stood. The only part of the great estate more or less intact is the gardener's house near the front gate. The entire property is on the National Register of Historic Places.

For many years the property was owned by a Christian missionary organization that slowly faded. Now the State of New Jersey, Bordentown, and the D&R Greenway Land Trust, an environmental organization, jointly own the site. It is quite wonderful that three different institutions could join forces in this endeavor. Otherwise, this historic site, the only open and unclaimed land in Bordentown, was going to be turned into warehouses and/or apartment buildings. D&R Greenway has taken on the responsibility of turning the gardener's house into a museum, which will be open to the public and managed by the Greenway. As I write this, D&R Greenway has already begun to renovate the gardener's house. Its shabby doors have been replaced by fine wooden ones, and what is being called "Bonaparte's Garden" is already planned and flourishing, with a fence around it.

The museum's contents will include artifacts found by the archeologists who conducted a dig at the site of the first palace. It is hoped that someday archeologists will conduct a similar survey of the site of the second home, which was given by Joseph Bonaparte to his grandson, Joseph, in 1839. He hoped the estate would remain in the family forever, but young Joseph didn't take care of it. It deteriorated rapidly, and eventually he sold off what he could of its contents, and it was torn down.

Joseph finally reunited with his wife in 1839 before dying in Florence in 1844. His more modest tomb is in Les Invalides in Paris along with the spectacular one of his brother.

Joseph's status in America was enhanced by the nature of his friends and visitors. Perhaps it was his position as a former king that made him especially popular with the ladies. In Bordentown he supported a mistress with whom he fathered two children and seems to have had children with other American women as well. There is no evidence, one way or the other, whether he provided for the welfare of his progeny when he left the United States for good in 1839.

But it was the distinguished people who visited his giant homes who put Point Breeze in competition with the White House as a center of American social life. This included distinguished foreigners. Frenchmen of distinction were invariably his guests when they visited the United States or were in exile. The Marquis de Lafayette, so important to America's victory over the British in the Revolutionary War, was twice Joseph's guest during his triumphal final tour of the United States in 1824. Though there is no hard evidence of this, some maintain that he was also visited by monarchist emissaries from Mexico offering him the Mexican crown. There seems to have been in Mexico a taste for rule by a European monarch, given that Maximilian, archduke of Austria, was declared emperor in 1864 (only to be executed by Republican forces in 1867), so perhaps Joseph was indeed sought after decades earlier. If so, it is clear that Bonaparte much preferred the luxury of living like a king to the responsibilities inherent in actually being one, so if indeed he was asked, one can imagine his politely declining the honor.

Distinguished Americans competed with one another for invitations to Joseph's palace-like homes, where they were waited upon by liveried servants. Americans of note who visited Point Breeze included Henry Clay, John Quincy Adams, Daniel Webster, James Monroe, and the Philadelphia banker Stephen Girard, of French origin and considered the richest man in the United States at that time. Members of the New Jersey State Legislature regularly visited him at his home. He was also visited by distinguished writers, artists, and naturalists. John James Audubon is believed to have drawn many of the sketches for his bird paintings while a guest of Joseph's. The presence of these visitors enhanced the importance of the site both nationally and internationally.

I hope the chapter on Washington's crossings and this one on Joseph Bonaparte's residences on the Delaware are ample examples of the history that lines this swift-flowing river. Other history of note unfolded on its banks. One might mention the serious consideration given to making Trenton the capital of the United States, and that Philadelphia, of course, actually served temporarily as the capital.

Bridges Not to
Be Missed

Is there a river anywhere with so many bridges and with such a great variety of them as the Delaware? Here I am only talking about the New Jersey bridges to Pennsylvania, not the New York bridges that also cross the river. While there is only one bridge from New Jersey to Delaware—the dual span Delaware Memorial Bridge—there are thirty-one vehicle and two pedestrian only New Jersey bridges that cross to Pennsylvania, plus seven railroad bridges. Virtually every town one comes to on the Jersey side of the river, no matter how tiny, seems to connect by bridge to the Pennsylvania side, usually to another town, creating a twin cities effect. The magazine *River Towns*, focused on the Delaware and its immediate surroundings, celebrates the river's bridges. For its winter 2020 issue it sponsored a photo essay on them.

There are two books on the bridges, one completely devoted to New Jersey's Delaware River bridges.[1] The other book, commenting on the extraordinary number of Delaware River bridges, sees them as "making New Jersey a vast open-air museum of structural art." It also refers to the bridges as "functional sculptures."[2]

This statement reminds us that bridges are architecture as much as they are engineering, often as beautiful as they are functional. In a book of mine, the great twentieth-century architect Mies van der Rohe describes the George Washington Bridge as "the most beautiful building" in New York City. The fact that Mies refers to the bridge as a "building" breaks down the false dichotomy between engineering and architecture.[3] Attractive bridges are clearly both. They are more than just convenient ways of crossing rivers.

The building of bridges on the Delaware occurred in concert with the ending of two industries. First, bridges drove ferries out of business, and some ferry owners actually sued for compensation, a few moderately succeeding. The other industry was the floating of large rafts of tree trunks downriver after they were harvested up North, en route to the industries of Trenton and Philadelphia. Early in American history, Philadelphia was the center of the shipbuilding industry and is often credited as the birthplace of the American Navy.

The rafts would not have easily passed through the stone supports of many of the bridges. Indeed, before the timber rafts were given up there had been a series of notable crashes into bridge supports. From an environmental point of view, it was a blessing that lumber rafting was brought to a conclusion. Because of their closeness to easy transport, the trees most often cut were on the banks of the river or at only a moderate distance inland. Gone was their value in moderating floods and curtailing erosion with their vast root systems, which ensured the effect of heavy rains on the banks of the Delaware and its tributaries were generally kept to the rivers and didn't cause flooding.

Characteristic of the Delaware River bridges is the great number that are free of tolls. For the most part, one doesn't pay tolls until Trenton, followed by Philadelphia—except for the I-80 and I-78 crossings and all those to the south. At first it was the owners of ferries, sometimes together with their towns, that raised the capital to build bridges and paid for them with the tolls charged.

Today's toll-free bridges mostly cross the northern part of the river, where it is narrower. They have a kind of homespun charm, enhanced by the fact that traffic is generally light. There's something charming about watching a single car slowly crossing a bridge—not the madness of hundreds of competing ones, often bumper-to-bumper.

Most of these northern bridges were purchased by a bi-state New Jersey-Pennsylvania agency, the Delaware River Joint Toll Bridge Commission, which made them toll free. The commission manages these bridges and keeps them in good repair. The twin-span Delaware Memorial Bridge is the responsibility of the Delaware River and Bay Authority, also a bi-state agency. Three bridges in Burlington County are under the control of a separate county bridge commission. Another four bridges crossing the Delaware to Philadelphia are under the authority of yet another organization, the Delaware River Port Authority.

Since most Delaware River bridges, especially the smaller ones, have walkways, one can truly enjoy the river and the bridges themselves by casually walking across any of them to Pennsylvania and, when desired, back to New Jersey, going both ways a pleasant and somewhat different adventure. Some sixteen were originally covered bridges made of wood that were swept away over the years, especially in the great storms of 1903 and 1955, when the river rose as high as 33.8 feet. The 1903 flood was known as the Pumpkin Flood. It took place in the month of October, just before pumpkins would have been harvested. The river tore into surrounding farms, freeing the pumpkins and adding to the impact of the wall of water, which made for quite a colorful and unusual sight. One of the main improvements in bridges that have helped them withstand floods has been raising the height of decks so that the water, no matter how high, is unable to reach them.

The 1841 flood was almost as bad as the 1903 and 1955 floods. A wall of water charging downriver and hitting the rectangular, boxlike structure of a covered bridge would inevitably tear it loose, while it would pass through the more filigree-like structure of a steel bridge, not to mention the strength of steel in withstanding the water. But it wasn't only floods that brought down covered bridges. Fierce winds were sometimes enough, and sometimes even fire, especially that caused by lightning. Centre Bridge, originating in Stockton and first built in 1814, was demolished in 1923 by a huge fire that injured fifteen firefighters. It reopened in 1927 as a steel bridge.

A destroyed covered bridge would sometimes float rapidly downriver and crash into the next covered bridge. This is what one did during the 1841 flood. Torn loose by the water, it sailed down the river and took out the New Hope-Lambertville Bridge. The very last of the Delaware covered bridges, with a slate roof, extended from Columbia, New Jersey, to Portland, Pennsylvania. It was destroyed by the 1955 flood. Indeed, there is a plaque mounted on the Portland side of the steel bridge that replaced it, apparently mounted there by the Boy Scouts, that reads: SITE OF THE LAST OF 16 COVERED BRIDGES THAT ONCE SPANNED THE DELAWARE—ERECTED

1831–1888/DESTROYED BY FLOOD AUG.-19-1955. The fifty-seven-year expanse of bridge-building includes the repairs and improvements often required by covered bridges, until they were replaced by steel ones.

An interesting aspect of early covered bridges is that, in winter, snow often had to be placed on the flooring so that sleighs pulled by horses could pass over them. There is irony here: the bridge was covered to keep it free of rain and snow, but under certain conditions snow was needed to get people across the river. Another interesting aspect is that the wood on the sides of covered bridges often was used to paint giant advertisements for a variety of products. One had COCA-COLA splashed on it in huge letters that spanned the river. That was back when coca, used to make cocaine, was part of the secret formula of Coke. But before you get upset and pour all your Coca-Cola down the drain so your children can't get at it, you should know that unprocessed coca leaves are no more stimulating than tea and are not in the least addictive. The Columbia to Portland wooden bridge had a huge advertisement painted across its full 775-foot length saying: PURE AND HARMLESS SOZODENT FOR THE TEETH AND BREATH. Sozodent was a popular toothpaste from mid to late nineteenth century. It was then discovered that it wasn't at all harmless to human health. One more thing about covered bridges: they were often called "kissing bridges." Couples went there because of the privacy they afforded.

There is one genuine covered bridge left in New Jersey, though it is not quite on the Delaware. It is in the hamlet of Sergeantsville, New Jersey (the first part of the name pronounced *surge*, not *sarge*), just east of downtown Stockton. Built in 1872, the eighty-four-foot Green Sergeant's Bridge fords Wickecheoke Creek, before it charges alongside and once powered the Prallsville Mills in Stockton and filled the D&R feeder, its excess pouring into the Delaware. The bridge has often needed repairs over the years. In 2013, a truck endeavoring to cross the river smashed into it. But as it has been with other injuries over the years, the bridge quickly made a comeback, enthusiastically supported by nearby residents who cherish it.

Technically, there is another New Jersey covered bridge in Cherry Hill, fifty-five feet long, that fords a branch of the Cooper River, but few consider it genuine because of its modern vintage and the sense that it was built, they feel, merely for decorative purposes, specifically to match a housing development across the road. Both the housing development and bridge were built by a Mr. Scarborough and named for him, which some see as

The Green Sergeants covered bridge in the hamlet of Sergeantsville, just outside of Stockton.

self-serving. One wonders whether, given enough time, it may take on some historical charm and significance.

If I had to pick my favorite bridges on the Delaware, they would be the two pedestrian/bikes-only ones, the first of which replaced that last covered bridge from Columbia, New Jersey, to Portland, Pennsylvania. It's four miles south of the Delaware Water Gap. Towards evening, folks walk their dogs across the bridge and young lovers embrace and kiss. A quarter mile downstream there is a second Columbia-Portland bridge, this one for vehicles.

The other pedestrian-only bridge is at Raven Rock. It passes from the Bull's Island section of the D&R Canal State Park (where the Delaware and Raritan Canal feeder begins) and crosses to Lumberville, Pennsylvania. It was once a wooden covered bridge and allowed vehicles, but after many flood disasters, it closed to traffic in 1944. The Delaware River Joint Toll Bridge Commission decided that there was no pressing need for a vehicle bridge at this point, so in 1947 the bridge reopened as a steel suspension bridge for pedestrians. It was built by Trenton's John A. Roebling's Sons Company. It is such a joy to walk or bike across a bridge without having to compete with automobiles and trucks, a great way to enjoy a river. One can only hope for

A Sunday crowd of hikers and bikers on the Raven Rock-Lumberville Bridge, closed to motor vehicles.

more pedestrian-only bridges. Local governments might consider that these bridges provide recreation opportunities at little cost and contribute to the health and well-being of citizens.

There are people who love the Raven Rock, New Jersey, to Lumberville, Pennsylvania, bridge even more than I do. These people live nearby and cross it regularly on foot or by bicycle. Others occasionally go even further, using the bridge for social occasions. Sure, why not party on the bridge? But get married on it? A double marriage no less? In two states?

That is exactly what two middle-age couples did on June 3, 2022. Three of the participants dated their friendship back to high school, and two of them had been neighbors and known each other since they were young children. The two couples had started double-dating two years before. One of the couples had a license from Pennsylvania and was, they hoped, marrying in that state, while the other was licensed in and believed they were marrying in New Jersey, though they stood just a few feet apart on the bridge. There is no state line sign on the bridge, but they had determined together what was likely the very center of the bridge by carefully counting bridge supports.

People walking across the bridge in their jeans and shorts came upon the two couples dressed in their wedding finery and respectfully paused and watched the event. The double wedding took some fifteen minutes and, when it was over, both couples walked to the Pennsylvania side with their officiants to have a drink at Lumberville's Bass Hotel. The next day there was a reception held for seventy-five people at the Rumson, New Jersey, home of the New Jersey celebrants.[4]

Of course, bridges can't all be pedestrian-only. But even bridges for automotive vehicles usually have, or should have, walkways. The new Scudder Falls Bridge has a walkway ten feet wide and connects the Delaware Canal towpath in Pennsylvania with the Delaware and Raritan Canal towpath in New Jersey. So, you can hike or bike one towpath, cross the bridge, and continue on the other towpath. This is one of seven such loop trails across the Delaware.

I don't believe any bridge should be built without the sightseeing and exercise potential of at least one walkway or bikeway. Unfortunately, one such bridge is the Verrazano, stretching from Staten Island to Brooklyn and restricted to automotive vehicles, with no walkways. Only once a year are "pedestrians" allowed on the bridge, the 50,000 participants in the New York City Marathon, whose race begins on the upper level of the bridge, temporarily closing it to traffic. Once all contestants have crossed the bridge, no one will run or walk it or, as in the case of some brave souls, cross it in a wheelchair, for another year. I can well imagine what an adventure it would be to hike or bike from Staten Island to Brooklyn. The Verrazano is the perfect embodiment of Robert Moses's philosophy, which always favored automotive vehicles to the exclusion of pedestrians. One wonders whether the fact that Moses never learned to drive influenced his attitude. One would think he would have favored pedestrians instead!

Thank goodness Moses had nothing to do with the bridges over the Delaware. I might add that the technology exists to remedy the lack of pedestrian walkways on those few bridges that do not have them. The basic procedure would be to cantilever out steel supports from the present bridge, which would be more than strong enough to support walkway/bikeways.

There is one bridge over the Delaware that is unlike all others today. Like many, Dingman's in far northern New Jersey was originally a ferry, and the bridge's curious full name is Dingman's Ferry Bridge. It was turned into a bridge by the ferry owners and is privately owned and maintained to this day, the only such bridge on the Delaware and one of the few in the United

States. When the Delaware River Joint Toll Bridge Commission attempted to buy it, its owners refused. They took pride in their bridge and they thought that by not selling, they could make more money over time by charging tolls.

It is a family business, passed down through generations. I wanted to get a picture of where and how the tolls are collected and it cost me $1 to cross to Pennsylvania and $1 to return—no E-Z Pass, cash only. I was lucky. Just a few weeks later the toll went up to $2 each way. The tolls are collected by an attendant or two, who normally are in a little shack on the Pennsylvania side and come out into the road to collect the toll. When I went there the toll collectors did not wear uniforms. They looked like they had come directly from home wearing exactly what they would wear cooking dinner or gardening. When I pulled up, they smiled and asked if there was anything they could help me with. Nobody was behind me and nobody was coming the other way, so we had a friendly chat. It was a charming experience. It felt so good to just slow down and escape into the past, away from cell phones and apps and social media. I think if I'm in that area again I might just cross the bridge and back for the sheer novelty of it. I hear that sometimes the bridge is used to move herds of cattle across the river, and a small toll paid for each animal. I'd sure like to see that. Even better would have been to be at the bridge when a bear crossed it one day. The bear did not pay a toll. A hearse crossed the bridge on one occasion and the toll-taker, while insisting no extra toll be paid for the coffin (as might be charged for a commercial vehicle, not to mention one with a body in it) thought there was something suspicious about the driver and insisted he open the coffin. He refused, but when she insisted, he opened it to reveal it was full of whiskey bottles. There ensued a long discussion arriving at an agreed upon toll.

Dingman's has a long history. Way back in 1775, Andrew Dingman built his family home on the Pennsylvania bank and gave it a name: Dingman's Choice. He renamed the house Dingman's Ferry after building docks on both sides of the river and going into the ferry business. Just beyond the dock on the New Jersey side is the Old Mine Road. There is a hamlet on the Pennsylvania side of the bridge that is also called Dingman's Ferry.

The ferry remained in operation off and on for well over one hundred years, and was guided across the river attached to a cable. But the ferry was slow, and people awaiting it on either bank would be frustrated by what could be an hour-long wait. During those years the Dingman family built a wooden bridge several times, including a covered one, but it was brought down by other covered bridges when they charged down the river

Collecting tolls on Dingman's Ferry Bridge, the only bridge in New Jersey still privately owned.

in storms. Another version of the bridge was literally lifted off its supports by fierce winds that blew it into the river. It is believed that, on yet another occasion, a tornado hit it. Every time the bridge was destroyed or in need of major repairs, the Dingmans went back to ferrying temporarily. But ferrying had its own challenges: chunks of ice in the river and the sudden appearance of log rafts that were not in complete control. The fact that the bridge is still called Dingman's Ferry Bridge, even though there is no ferry and it is no longer owned by the Dingman family, makes it seem as if its owners don't wish to depart from history by dropping the word "ferry." Finally, in 1900 the steel bridge that's stands there today was built. It was assembled using three spans from a five-span abandoned railroad bridge taken down elsewhere in Pennsylvania.

The bridge is open all year, twenty-four seven. No trucks or buses are allowed. One can combine a visit there with a visit to the tri-state rock just a few miles north on the New Jersey side.

Dingman's Ferry has another function in history. When New Jersey was two royal colonies, East and West Jersey, the diagonal line that separated them began at Little Egg Harbor in Ocean County and ended at the very spot that would eventually be the Jersey side of Dingman's Ferry.

The bridge at Riegelsville, next to where the Musconetcong River enters the Delaware, is worth mentioning because it has Roebling wire rope and was, in part designed by John Roebling, though others were involved. Roebling wire was used in many bridges that the Roeblings themselves did not build, including the George Washington Bridge. John Roebling was, however, the builder of a wire rope aqueduct over the Delaware for the Delaware and Hudson Canal, twenty miles north of the New Jersey border in New York State. The aqueduct was built in 1849 and is 535 feet long. It is the oldest wire suspension bridge in the United States still extant, built long before the Brooklyn Bridge, the project which gained the Roeblings fame. After giving up its function as an aqueduct, it became a vehicle bridge and then a pedestrian-only bridge. After restoration by the National Park Service, it is now a vehicle bridge again.

I want to mention one other bridge and issue a warning. It's the bridge that crosses the river between Washington's Crossing, New Jersey, and Washington's Crossing, Pennsylvania. I think it's the narrowest two-lane bridge I've ever been on, and it doesn't have a walkway. The original bridge was destroyed in the 1941 flood, so there was plenty of time and technology to build an adequately sized vehicle bridge. Before mounting it, pull in your mirrors if you can and drive as slowly as possible. Even so, the number of people who lose mirrors on that bridge or get scratches on their car is legion. Though I drove as carefully as I could, I chipped the paint of my passenger-side mirror anyway while striking the side of the bridge. Better than the head-on collision I was trying to avoid, I figured. Frankly, the two states should set up red and green lights, allowing passage in only one direction at a time. Perhaps the bridge is purposely so narrow as a means of reminding us of George Washington's trials and tribulations long ago in the waters below.

Life on the Bay

Delaware Bay is part of the 331-mile Delaware River, whether one is counting the river from its northern origins as I do, or, as seagoing vessels naturally prefer, from the fourteen-mile-wide entrance to the bay between New Jersey's Cape May and Delaware's Cape Henlopen. Considerable numbers of oceangoing ships pass through Delaware Bay en route to and from the industries of Wilmington and Philadelphia. Some, entering or leaving the bay may then pass through the Chesapeake and Delaware Canal, which connects Delaware Bay and Chesapeake Bay, Philadelphia and Baltimore, by an inland route that saves many miles.

The shore of Delaware Bay, at least on the Jersey side, is often referred to as New Jersey's "Forgotten Coast" because it is so absent of people, towns, and industry. The bay actually begins or ends on the western side of Cape May, so Cape May is, in part, on Delaware Bay though mostly on the Atlantic. The river becomes an estuary at tidal Trenton and is thought to continue through the bay, though by then it is largely ocean saltwater. It is difficult to determine the length of the bay because the estuary broadens the farther south and then southeast it flows, so just where the estuary ends and the bay begins must be decided somewhat arbitrarily. Some sources consider the bay to be 42 miles in length, others 52. The Delaware River Bay Commission uses the figure 48.2 river miles, which I suppose may be considered the official dimension. As for the width at its widest point, the commission uses the figure of 28.25 miles.

However its dimensions are calculated, a small piece of the bay is at the southwestern corner of Salem County, and the great majority of it is south of or under Cumberland County. Much of its New Jersey shoreline is either marshes or sandy beaches, though both are already changing as the ocean rises, threatening homes built near the bay. The beaches were once fairly popular, with small towns and vacation homes adjoining them that included boardwalks, shops, and restaurants. Today they are largely abandoned, and the towns generally gone with scarcely a trace, the roads to them largely obliterated. For years the wreckage of boats was seen along the bay beaches, but eventually they disappeared too. Much of this bay civilization was destroyed in 1950 by a fierce storm that swept it away, in the process killing at least fourteen people, a number of them Boy Scouts who were camping there. The waters of Delaware Bay are normally quite still with no surf, almost like a lake. But as the storm of 1950 hit, the water in the bay was ominously sucked out to sea, only to come roaring back as a giant tidal wave or tsunami. Those who have written about this event sometimes use one term, sometimes the other. Given that the water was sucked out to sea and then returned as a devastating wave, I would favor the second term, though unlike most tsunamis there was no known precipitating event such as an undersea earthquake or volcanic eruption.

Sea Breeze was once a popular bay beach town, so popular that it was a regular steamboat stop, bringing boatfuls of people from Philadelphia and Wilmington. Many came to stay in a large luxury hotel. The town had even built an elaborate sea wall to protect itself from a possible rogue wave, but the wall was not only surpassed but destroyed by the 1950 tidal wave and the hotel and town with it. Much of the Cumberland shore is a place of former or all but obliterated towns.

The decline of bay beaches contributed, in part, to the already great popularity of the forty-four beaches on the Atlantic. Today one may walk along bay beaches for miles without seeing anyone, or perhaps just the occasional person, offering a somewhat unique and solitary experience to the more adventurous among us. Some refer to these beaches as ghost beaches. Nevertheless, should you wish to be on a beach absent great crowds, often your very own beach, the bay beaches await you. They are also ideal for young children because there are normally no waves to knock them over.

These essentially abandoned beaches are nevertheless symptomatic of the poverty of Cumberland, which is routinely listed as New Jersey's poorest or next-to-poorest county, switching places from year to year with Salem County. However, in studies of health and life expectancy in New Jersey's counties, Cumberland routinely comes in last. And mediocre schools, unemployment, poverty, and poor health conditions appear to rise in the county the closer one gets to the bay, partly because of the collapse of the industries that once made the bay's shore a prosperous place.

Among the poor in Cumberland County living near the bay are a disproportionate number of African Americans. They were once reasonably prosperous, working in the sea industries typical of the bay: oysters and sturgeon caviar. One thing we tend to forget is that slavery existed throughout New Jersey, especially in South Jersey, until the end of the Civil War. When Lincoln issued the Emancipation Proclamation in 1863 it referred only to Confederate states, not Union states, especially those close to Washington such as Maryland and Delaware, so that they would remain loyal to the Union. Slavery persisted in New Jersey for similar reasons. Had Maryland, in particular, not remained in the union till the end of the Civil War, Washington might have been surrounded by the Confederacy, with Maryland on one side and Virginia on the other. It's difficult to accept that a chunk of South Jersey would be below the Mason Dixon line if the line went straight across and that slavery persisted in the state even after the Emancipation Proclamation and until the end of the Civil War. One would like to think of New Jersey as more enlightened.

It is likely that some African Americans presently living in southern Cumberland County are the descendants of enslaved people who continued to live in the area after the Civil War. Sometimes when I am in Cumberland County close to the bay it feels like I'm actually in 1930s Depression America, perhaps in rural Mississippi. This was not always the case. Until the 1950s, Delaware Bay was the oyster capital of New Jersey and likely the most productive oyster grounds in America. At its height, oystering produced as much as one million bushels per year. One can sense this by the huge piles of oyster shells found in various parts of Cumberland County, lying there as if mysteriously left by practitioners of some ancient religious rite or visitors from another planet. One rather expects to see archeologists working in the area. The piles of shells are nevertheless a remnant of what

A huge pile of oyster shells in the aptly named former town of Shell Pile, New Jersey.

was once an affluent part of New Jersey that disappeared along with the oyster industry.

Until recently, there was actually a town named Shell Pile, which is often referred to as "the loneliest place in New Jersey." It was slowly abandoned and then largely disintegrated, leaving scant evidence it had ever existed, except for a handsome sign that ironically says:

WELCOME TO THE VILLAGE OF SHELL PILE, A CLEAN COMMUNITY. It may be clean but, essentially, it isn't there—except for the piles of oyster shells that gave the town its name and a house or two that look so abandoned it's hard to believe even the poorest Americans could be living in them.

Another town with the equally improbable name of Bivalve is still technically, but just barely, alive. It lost its post office in 1971 and since then has been officially linked to nearby Port Norris, as in a sense it always was. (Shell Pile was once referred to as South Port Norris.) Shell Pile and Bivalve have always been considered part of Greater Port Norris. When the oyster industry was in its prime in the 1950s, Port Norris was commonly referred to as the Oyster Capital of the World. Some regarded it as the wealthiest town in New Jersey, with a sizeable quantity of millionaires. Today, it is simply a

A house, actually occupied, that remains in Shell Pile, New Jersey.

quiet, modest, poor place of no particular distinction, representative of what once was Cumberland County and what became of it.

A bivalve is a shellfish with a hinge and two internal valves though which it feeds by filtering sustenance out of the water. Mussels, clams, scallops, and oysters are bivalves. The town of Bivalve was the center of the oyster industry. Imagine living in a town with the name Bivalve! Rutgers University has a research station at Bivalve, and it is a standing joke among university faculty, except those researching the science of the sea, that if you get into some trouble, you will be exiled to work at Bivalve.

The industry broke down after 95 percent of oysters in the area were destroyed by a parasite, and it is only now making feeble efforts at recovery. One way to enhance oyster production is by throwing those shells just mentioned into the bay, for baby oysters to attach themselves to. This is happening and those vast piles are declining and oysters increasing. I might mention that what is happening in the bay is part of a wider movement to reestablish the oyster industry along other parts of New Jersey's ocean or ocean-connected estuaries.

Another once prominent sea creature of the bay is the Atlantic sturgeon, which comes into Delaware Bay and the lower estuary to spawn. It is a unique species, known nowhere else in the world. Some 400 sturgeon fishermen were headquartered in what is now the town of Bayside, in Greenwich Township, at the western extreme of Cumberland County. Bayside was originally called "Caviar" because of the abundant roe harvested from female sturgeon that made the town the caviar capital of the United States, considered by some the caviar capital of the world. In any case, it was a boomtown. At the height of the industry in the 1890s, fifteen train cars of caviar and smoked sturgeon were being shipped to New York City each day, on rails laid just for this purpose. Fortunes were made. It was the New Jersey equivalent of the California Gold Rush.

We normally associate caviar with Russia, but regardless of who had more, the United States definitely exported more. But Sturgeon, which sometimes reach 800 pounds, began to be affected by the pollution that became a feature of the Delaware, especially in the bay. Worse was the killing of female sturgeon, just to get caviar eggs, that primarily put the fish on the Endangered Species List in 2012. There were an estimated 180,000 sturgeon in Delaware Bay before 1890, so many that people used to joke that one could walk across the bay on their backs.

By the early twentieth century, however, because of pollution and overfishing, their decline was extreme. Today, there are believed to be no more than 300–500 sturgeon that come into Delaware Bay to spawn. Sturgeon, believed to be one of the oldest species on our planet, present when the dinosaurs were here, has become a key example of the ruin we human beings have visited upon our planet.

However dim this present view of Delaware Bay may be—especially the near disappearance of oysters and surgeon—there is what could be another equally great threat. The beaches of the bay, right up to Reeds Beach on the west or Delaware Bay side of Cape May, have been essential to migrating birds, especially the red knot but also ruddy turnstones, sanderlings, and sandpipers. The red knots travel each year from the southern tip of South America to the Arctic and back again when the seasons change, some 9,300 miles each way. Ornithologists tell us that, like other long-distance migrating birds, the red knots have a divided or dual brain, half of which can be shut down so they can rest and sleep while the other half concentrates on flying. They can also close one eye on the side of their head to sleep and have two sets of lungs. Coming north, they actually fly some five-and-a-half days and nights nonstop to land on Delaware Bay beaches, halfway to their ultimate destination. All those days without eating anything and faced with dehydration and exhaustion! Having lost half their weight, they feed and fatten on the eggs of horseshoe crabs for a couple of weeks. Then, well nourished, they take off for the Arctic where they will produce their young. Clearly, they prefer the cool summers of the Arctic north and the cool extreme southern hemisphere summers and are willing to do whatever it takes to get from one place to the other, year after year.

It is a wonder of nature that the birds arrive in spring on Delaware Bay beaches just as horseshoe crabs come ashore on the tides. The crabs stay ashore (just barely) on the beach or in shallow water for most of the month of May. The male crabs fertilize the eggs and gather round the females to protect them from the birds, but there are enough eggs for the horseshoe crabs to reproduce and the birds to fatten themselves on. The horseshoe crab is considered a keystone species, one that other species depend on for their survival.

Horseshoe crabs slowly coming ashore in Delaware Bay to reproduce, soon to meet up with migrating birds. Photo by Jan van der Kam. From *Life along the Delaware Bay: Cape May, Gateway to a Million Shore Birds* (Rutgers University Press, 2012). Reprinted by permission of Lawrence Niles.

Migrating birds feeding on horseshoe crab eggs on Reeds Beach, located on Delaware Bay on the west side of Cape May. Photo by Jan van der Kam. From *Life along the Delaware Bay: Cape May, Gateway to a Million Shore Birds* (Rutgers University Press, 2012). Reprinted by permission of Lawrence Niles.

The relationship between the horseshoe crabs and the birds is nature at its most wonderful, a ritual dating back, as does the spawning of the sturgeon, well over 400 million years to the time of the dinosaurs. The west side of Cape May is a birder's paradise, though bird-watching is not something most people associate with the cape. Many of us are familiar with the Victorian architecture and the sparkling Cape May "diamonds" (actually quartz pebbles) on the beach. But in certain seasons it is birders who dominate the scene. There is even a birder's lookout high up in the Cape May lighthouse.

All would be well (the birds fed and the female horseshoe crabs, each carrying some 80,000 eggs, reproducing adequately) if it were not for the intrusion of our own species, which has tended to regard horseshoe crabs as ugly, useless creatures (sometimes disparagingly referred to as "living fossils"), cluttering the bay and of no use to anyone. Admittedly people generally do not eat horseshoe crabs, and they are not the most attractive of sea creatures, so, for years, farmers were invited to come to bay beaches to pick up as many horseshoe crabs as they could fit in their trucks, only to take them back to their farms and grind them up for fertilizer or to feed livestock. It is estimated that 2.5 million horseshoe crabs, largely in New Jersey but up into New England as well, had been killed by 1997. Fortunately, by 2006, the killing of horseshoe crabs was forbidden by law in New Jersey. However, in 2022 the Atlantic States Fisheries Commission awarded permission to fisherman to again use horseshoe crabs and their eggs for bait.

This is a monstrous oversight, made worse because fishermen often take horseshoe crabs as they come ashore, before the females have been able to deposit their eggs in the sand and the males to fertilize them. Thus, not only is the population of live horseshoe crabs reduced, but many have no progeny succeeding them.[1]

Small wonder that the number of horseshoe crabs on the bay continues to decline, as have the birds that depend on them for their migratory survival. A few years back there were 1.5 million migrating birds on Cumberland County beaches. Now there are half that many, if that. Some sources insist that the decline of red knots in particular has been as high as 80 percent, though the figure of 50 percent is probably more accurate. Either way, this is a dramatic example of the diminution of species that scientists cite as evidence that our planet is in deep trouble—but this one could be remedied by changing human behavior at little or no cost. Also, despite all the losses, Delaware Bay is still the number-one site for horseshoe crabs, not only in New Jersey but in the world. We should mention that horseshoe crabs are not crabs but more closely related to spiders and scorpions—which I suppose makes them even less attractive to people and easy to eliminate without much thought by those unaware of their value. On the other hand, their presumed ugliness would seem to be a blessing because most people reject them as food, though there are countries in Asia that do not share this prejudice, so this is yet another means to reduce horseshoe numbers.

The survival and flourishing of horseshoe crabs is threatened in another way—but here in a necessary cause. The milky blue blood of horseshoe crabs is used in laboratories to test the safety of vaccines—something in these days of COVID and likely pandemics of the future that is essential. Half the horseshoe crabs harvested by fishermen are sold to laboratories, where some of their blood is extracted. It is a critical component of efforts to ensure vaccines are not in any way contaminated. The horseshoe crabs are then returned to the sea unharmed, at least according to pharmaceutical companies. Conservationists tend to disagree. They point out that 15–30 percent of the horseshoe crabs die in the process. Perhaps another means will be adopted by pharmaceutical companies in the future but, until it is, this is likely to remain an essential use that is necessary and far more respectful of the lives of horseshoe crabs than, say, grinding them up for fertilizer.[2] Indeed, pharmaceutical companies already have an artificial substance in its preliminary stages that may prove to be as effective as horseshoe crab blood in detecting defects in vaccines.

Luckily, consciousness of the value of horseshoe crabs is growing. For example, volunteer groups have in recent years patrolled bay beaches as the migratory birds depart to right horseshoe crabs turned over by the tides and propel or carry them back toward the water. The crabs are usually incapable of turning themselves back over. Following a few days stranded on the beach, they will dry out and die. That is, if they are not first devoured by migrating birds who will peck at crabs that are turned over and vulnerable.

But when horseshoe crabs are allowed to do their job, there is still danger along the Delaware Bay. Climate change is real and happening now; the seas are already rising. The saltwater kills trees and shrubs, which are then replaced by more and more marshes, which in effect makes it difficult to discern just where the land ends and the bay begins, not to mention that the marshes themselves are steadily being driven inland by the rising waters. This has greatly reduced the production of salt hay, once used in the making of mattresses but today mostly sold by plant nurseries for agricultural purposes such as mulching.

The marshes and water are coming closer to the remaining towns near the bay. Dunes, which protect against storms, are also washing away, leading to more coastal flooding and erosion. A notable example of this is Cumberland County's Gandy's Beach, which is also the name of a settlement. Water from the bay has moved so rapidly inland that there is no longer a beach, and the marshy shoreline is 500 feet inland from where it was not long ago. Since the town is only at an elevation of three feet, it is easy to imagine it becoming overrun by the waters of the bay in the not-so-distant future. Even more ominously, the Rutgers Marine Field Station believes the sea level is rising as fast in New Jersey as anywhere else in the world. In this respect, the state is already experiencing climate change. It serves as a reminder that, south of the Watchung Mountains, where the glaciers once terminated, New Jersey is largely flat and low-lying. The Pine Barrens, which occupies almost one-fourth of the state and is its lowest-lying portion, will likely be submerged first.

Despite the fact that Cumberland County is little known or explored by most New Jerseyans, especially as one gets closer to the bay, it has history and civilization. Founded in 1685, Greenwich Township was important in American history for reasons other than the caviar harvested in Caviar-Bayhead, one of its dependencies. I should point out that unlike Greenwich, Connecticut, the Cumberland County Greenwich has long been pronounced "Green witch." This was originally for patriotic reasons: its citizens did not wish to be associated with what they considered English pretensions in the pronunciation of Greenwich. More important, Greenwich was the site at which a second tea party took place on December 22, 1774, a year after the more famous Boston one. The tea was stored in the basement of a Loyalist and was about to be shipped to Philadelphia. Some forty patriots, as in Boston dressed as indigenous warriors, did not dump the tea in Delaware Bay or its tributary, the Cohansey River, but burned it instead. One of their number was Richard Howell, who, after America gained its independence, was the third governor of New Jersey. In 1908, the Cumberland County Historical Society erected a monument to the tea burning in Greenwich at Main Street and Market Square.

There is also important history nearby in Bridgeton, the county seat, which has its own liberty bell proudly kept in the county courthouse. The bell, cast in 1763, is taken out and rung on occasions of national importance, beginning with the arrival of the news that American independence had been declared in Philadelphia in 1776. So, by no means is Cumberland County all beaches, marshes, and abandoned towns. For example, its main city, Vineland, is a major agricultural center with some 61,000 people. During World Wat II it was an essential food-processing center, supplemented by the nearby Seabrook Farms which were largely staffed by interned Japanese Americans. Remarkably, Vineland is also New Jersey's largest city in total area.

Another example of civilization in Cumberland County is the SS *Atlantus*. Just off Sunset Beach, close to the southern tip of the Delaware Bay side of Cape May, a concrete World War I vessel's wreckage still protrudes from the water after all these years. Visitors are to be found on the beach staring at it when the weather is good. In a sense it sums up Delaware Bay: not just wild but historic.

And the same might be said about the Delaware River and this book in general—or such has been my intention. The river is as untamed and natural as it is the scene of memorable historic events and personages. These things do not normally go together, but at the Delaware they do. I announced at this book's beginning that I wished to attract the reader to New Jersey's other shore. There is nothing wrong with what most New Jerseyans and people who live in our part of the country consider *the* Jersey Shore on the Atlantic, but those not familiar with this other shore are missing out on much that would bring pleasure to their lives. It would be a source of pride for me were this book to play a small part in attracting them there.

Acknowledgments

I've written a number of books, but I can't recall one with which I have been so grateful for the help of others as in the present case. That may be because, while I have always loved the Delaware and its immediate environment, I didn't begin this book as an expert but only as an admirer of my subject. Appearing below are the most important of my "co-authors," whose kindness and generosity was boundless. There were others, but were I to include everyone who helped and taught me, this section of the book would be longer than any of its chapters. I have thanked the others personally.

Kate Schmidt of the Delaware River Basin Authority helped me extensively when there were things I could not find out however much I tried.

James Lewis, of the North Jersey History and Genealogy Center of the Morristown and Morris Township Public Library, was tireless in securing books and information that would otherwise have been unavailable to me.

Robert and Linda Barth, long associated with the Canal Society of New Jersey, were tireless in their efforts to educate me on New Jersey's canals and their relationship to the Delaware River. Bob told me things not available elsewhere, and Linda helped in every way, including editing and correcting my errors, both factual and grammatical, throughout the book. The author of nine New Jersey-oriented books, she was instrumental in making my book a much better read. Bob's knowledge of canals stems in part from positions he has held, such as president of the Canal Society of New Jersey and vice president of the American Canal Society.

Ron Rice, also associated with the Canal Society of New Jersey, constantly sent me information on the canals and was instrumental in getting me to plane 9W and in setting up my meeting with Jim Lee Jr. and Jim Lee III. The Lees, like their father and grandfather, Jim Lee, were as hospitable as they were knowledgeable, and not just me but everyone in New Jersey owes the Lee family a lot.

Historian Jim Turk was instrumental in introducing me to aspects of the estuary and bay, especially the Finn's Point National Cemetery, which we visited together.

Brad Fay, then with the D&R Greenway Land Trust, was tireless in informing me on aspects of my project that had escaped my attention.

Charlie Groth and Steve Meserve took me under their wings to teach me about the Lewis Island Fishery. Charlie's book, *Another Haul*, was a significant influence.

Jim and Dawn McCreary and Judith Gauntt took me out to Burlington Island and instructed me on its curious history.

Todd Tersigni, mayor of Phillipsburg, helped me find the overgrown entrance to the Morris Canal on the Delaware River.

John Hutchison and Jim Amon, at different times directors of the D&R Canal Commission, were generous with their time and abundant with their information, as were Patricia Kallesser and Sid Cash of the D&R State Park Commission.

Doug Kiovsky and Steve Lederman of the Bordentown Historical Society took considerable time helping me understand Joseph Bonaparte's estates at Point Breeze, steering me through the forest to find the scant remains of Bonaparte's second house, and helping me to get permission to use the watercolor of the house from the Joslyn Museum of Omaha, Nebraska.

Tracy Carluccio of the Delaware Riverkeeper Network patiently explained to me the mission of the Riverkeepers while teaching me a good deal about the issue of floods on the river and how best to contain them. From her I learned that not taking down trees close to or at riverside can have as much, or more, to do with preventing floods as building dams because of the immense amounts of water their roots absorb.

Rick Epstein of Frenchtown guided me about that town with his customary enthusiasm.

Teri Watson, of the Bayshore Center at Bivalve, was my key source for the great storm of 1950.

Larry Niles was instrumental to my obtaining the pictures on Reeds Beach demonstrating just how horseshoe crabs and migrating birds relate to one another.

Fred Eisinger, of the Lambertville Historical Society, toured the town with me in the aftermath of Hurricane Ida, pointing out the most serious wreckage caused by the storm. It was from Fred I learned that tributaries, no matter how small, can be just as dangerous, if not more so, than major rivers.

Andras Fekete, the former manager of environmental services at the State Department of Transportation, was immensely helpful in briefing me on the Delaware early in my research.

Heather Hardwick, a former student, was instrumental to my understanding of the Cumberland County/Delaware Bay area.

Henri Schepens, mayor of Milford, New Jersey, helped me understand the presence of the cacti growing in the rocks outside Milford, New Jersey.

Angus Gillespie, friend, colleague, and my coauthor on another book, seemed to run a "clipping service," keeping me up to date on Delaware River affairs, while he and his wife, Rowena, were immensely helpful with the technical aspects of publishing a book these days—how to submit a manuscript, for example—which are significantly different from my previous experiences.

I am grateful to Michael Siegel, cartographer at Rutgers University, for the splendid maps, one that locates all the key places discussed in this book and another the New Jersey canals.

David Turner heroically went up in his 1941 (eighty-two-year-old) Piper Cub and took the lovely picture of the Delaware Water Gap that adorns the cover of this book.

Peter Mickulas, executive editor at Rutgers University Press, believed in this book, suggested important improvements, and gave me much intellectual and emotional support. He deserves much credit for the final version.

Finally, and most of all, I want to thank my wife, Patricia Ard, who constantly fed me information, from every media source, on an inexhaustible range of Delaware River–related topics.

Notes

Introduction

1　April Bernard and Luc Sante, *New Jersey: An American Portrait* (Dallas: Taylor Publishing, 1988).

Chapter 1　The Joy of a River

1　In 1966, John Cunningham wrote a book titled *New Jersey: America's Main Road* (New York: Doubleday). He mentioned that New Jersey is sometimes referred to as the Corridor State but went on to argue that it is, of course, so much more.

Chapter 2　The Delaware and New Jersey Geography

1　Steven M. Richman, *The Bridges of New Jersey: Portraits of Garden State Crossings* (New Brunswick, NJ: Rutgers University Press, 2005), xii.
2　*Guide to the Records of the New York and New Jersey Boundary Disputes* (Newark: New Jersey Historical Society, 2004). New Jersey had to fight to be included in what was originally called simply "The Port of New York."

Chapter 3　Islands in the Stream

1　Charlie Groth, *Another Haul: Narrative Stewardship and Cultural Sustainability at the Lewis Family Fishery* (Jackson: University Press of Mississippi, 2019).
2　John McPhee, *The Founding Fish* (New York: Farrar, Strauss and Giroux, 2002).
3　Bill Barlow, "The History of Submarine Warfare off the Jersey Coast," WHHY PBS, October 4, 2018, https://whyy.org/articles/the-history-of-submarine-warfare -off-the-jersey-coast/.
4　Laura M. Lee and Brendan Mackie, *Fort Delaware* (Charleston, SC: Arcadia Publishing, 2010).

5 The Emancipation Proclamation of 1863 had something to do with the breakdown of prisoner exchanges. It produced desperation in the slaveholding South and less willingness to negotiate with the North about anything.

6 "Escape from Fort Delaware," by Tracey Bryant, *University of Delaware Research* 2, no. 2, https://www1.udel.edu/researchmagazine/issue/vol2_no2_security /escape_from_fort_delaware.html.

7 These facts are asserted in an unpublished essay titled "New Jersey, the Last Northern State to End Slavery," by Noelle Lorraine Williams, director of the African American History Program, New Jersey Historical Commission.

8 Gail F. Safian, *Slavery in New Jersey: A Troubled History* (Maplewood, NJ: Durando-Hedden House, 2019).

9 Andrew Zwicker, "All Kidding Aside, It's Time to Put Central Jersey on the Map," New Jersey.com, October 20, 2022, https://www.nj.com/opinion/2022/10 /all-kidding-aside-its-time-to-put-central-jersey-on-the-map-opinion.html.

10 Works Progress Administration, *Stories of New Jersey* (New York: M. Barrows and Co., 1938), 82.

Chapter 4   The Delaware Water Gap and the Old Mine Road

1 Lauren Obiso, *Delaware Water Gap Recreation Area* (Charleston, SC: Arcadia Publishing, 2009), 9.

2 Steve Novak, "Gap in State's Resume—a National Park—Soon to Be Filled," *Star Ledger* (Newark, NJ), February 16, 2020, A17. See also Jason Nark, "Proposal Would Give N.J., Pa. First National Park," *Star Ledger* (Newark, NJ), November 7, 2021, A19.

3 Novak, "Gap in State's Resume."

4 Steve Novak, "National Park Idea Hits Rocky Patch," *The Star Ledger*, May 1, 2022, A17, 19.

5 Don and Marietta Dorfinger, *River Towns of the Delaware Water Gap* (Charleston, SC: Arcadia Publishing, 2017).

6 For an excellent book on hiking the Appalachian Trail, see Kristi M. Fondren, *Walking on the Wild Side: Long-Distance Hiking on the Appalachian Trail* (New Brunswick, NJ: Rutgers University Press, 2015).

7 Amelia Stickney Decker, *That Ancient Trail: The Old Mine Road* (Trenton, NJ: Petty Printing, 1942). See also C. G. Hine, *The Old Mine Road* (New Brunswick, NJ: Rutgers University Press, 1963). Facsimile edition of the first part of Hine's privately published *History and Legend, Fact, Fancy and Romance of the Old Mine Road, Kingston, N.Y., to the Mine Holes of Pahaquarry* (1909).

8 For a summary of the "Walking Treaty," see https://en.wikipedia.org/wiki /Walking_Purchase#cite_note-Gilbert-2. See also *Encyclopaedia Britannica*, "Walking Purchase," updated August 18, 2023, https://www.britannica.com/event /Walking-Purchase; Tim Hayburn, "Walking Purchase," *The Encyclopedia of Greater Philadelphia*, 2015, https://philadelphiaencyclopedia.org/essays/walking -purchase/.

9 "Was the Revolutionary War Hero Casimir Pulaski Intersex?," *Smithsonian Magazine*, April 9, 2019, https://www.smithsonianmag.com/smart-news/was -revolutionary-war-hero-casimir-pulaski-intersex-180971907/.

Chapter 5 The Dam That Was Never Built

1 Richard C. Albert, *Damming the Delaware: The Rise and Fall of Tocks Island Dam* (University Park: Penn State University Press, 1987).
2 Frank T. Dale, *Delaware Diary: Episodes in the Life of a River* (New Brunswick, NJ: Rutgers University Press, 1996), 151.
3 Dale, *Delaware Diary*, 155.
4 Albert, *Damming the Delaware*, 123.
5 Elizabeth Kolbert, "Testing the Waters: Should the Natural World Have Legal Rights?" *New Yorker*, April 18, 2022, 16–20.

Chapter 6 The River and the Canals

1 Tim Roth, of the Canal Society of New Jersey, in a program sponsored by the Chatham Historical Society on March 20, 2022, titled "The Morris Canal: Northern New Jersey's Water Highway."
2 Richard F. Veit, *The Old Canals of New Jersey* (Little Falls: New Jersey Geographical Press, 1963), 82.
3 Frances Trollope, *Domestic Manners of the Americans* (1832; repr., New York: Vintage Books, 1960), 347.
4 See Elizabeth G. C. Menzies, *Passage between Rivers: A Portfolio of Photographs with a History of the Delaware and Raritan Canal* (New Brunswick, NJ: Rutgers University Press, 1976).
5 "Delay on Delaware-Raritan Canal Assailed as Adding to War Perils," *New York Times*, February 15, 1942, F20.

Chapter 7 The Delaware Riviera

1 Renee Kirluk-Hill, "Lambertville Is One of *Forbes*' 15 Prettiest Towns in America," *Hunterdon County Democrat,* August 20, 2013, https://www.nj.com /hunterdon-county-democrat/2013/08/lambertville_is_one_of_forbes.html.

Chapter 8 Washington's Crossing(s)

1 Often the figure 5,000 and even 5,400 is used to describe Washington's army at the Christmas Crossing. These figures include units located elsewhere and not able to cross the Delaware or get to Trenton on time.
2 Michael Robbins, "Behind the Lines: the Durham Boat," *Military History Quarterly*, January 2015, https://www.historynet.com/behind-lines-durham-boat/.
3 The cover is from the *New Yorker*'s November 1, 2021, edition.
4 For a concise and well-written description of Washington and his army's critical activities from December 25 to January 3, see Clay Craighead, *The Ten Crucial Days*, published by Washington's Crossing State Park, Titusville, New Jersey, in 2011.

Chapter 9 Napoleon's Brother on the Banks of the Delaware

1 See Patricia Tyson Stroud, *The Man Who Had Been King: The American Exile of Napoleon's Brother Joseph* (Philadelphia: University of Pennsylvania, 2005), 22.

2 Owen Connelly, *The Gentle Bonaparte: A Biography of Joseph, Napoleon's Elder Brother* (New York: Macmillan, 1968), 25.
3 Richard F. Veit, professor of anthropology at Monmouth University, excavated the site of the first Joseph Bonaparte house with colleagues, students, and volunteers in 2020.

Chapter 10   Bridges Not to Be Missed

1 Frank T. Dale, *Bridges over the Delaware River* (New Brunswick, NJ: Rutgers University Press, 2003).
2 Stephen M. Richman, *The Bridges of New Jersey: Portraits of Garden State Crossings* (New Brunswick, NJ: Rutgers University Press, 2005), 4.
3 Michael Aaron Rockland, *The George Washington Bridge: Poetry in Steel*, revised and expanded ed. (New Brunswick, NJ: Rutgers University Press, 2020), 77.
4 Tammy La Gorce and Vincent Malozzi, "Combining Two Weddings in Different States," *Star Ledger* (Newark, NJ), July 17, 2022, 16.

Chapter 11   Life on the Bay

1 Deborah Cramer, "When the Horseshoe Crabs Are Gone, We'll Be in Trouble, *New York Times*, February 18, 2023, A1.
2 Michael Saul Warren, "Vaccine's Unlikely Star," *Star Ledger* (Newark, NJ), February 5, 2021, A1.

Selected Bibliography

Albert, Richard. *Damming the Delaware: The Rise and Fall of Tocks Island Dam.* University Park: Penn State University Press, 1987.

Barth, Linda J. *The Delaware and Raritan Canal.* Charleston, SC: Arcadia Publishers, 2002.

Bernard, April, and Luc Sante. *New Jersey: An American Portrait.* Dallas, TX: Taylor Publishing, 1988.

Bonk, David. *Trenton and Princeton 1776–77: Washington Crosses the Delaware.* New York: Osprey Press, 2009.

Burger, Joanna, Amanda Dey, and Lawrence Niles, with photographs by Jan van de Kam. *Life along the Delaware Bay: Cape May, Gateway to a Million Shorebirds.* New Brunswick, NJ: Rutgers University Press, 2012.

Chinici, R. Curt. *Stories from Raven Rock, New Jersey.* Charleston, SC: The History Press, 2012.

Connelly, Owen. *The Gentle Bonaparte: A Biography of Joseph, Napoleon's Elder Brother.* New York: Macmillan, 1968.

Cunningham, John. *New Jersey: America's Main Road.* New York: Doubleday, 1966.

Dale, Frank. *Bridges over the Delaware River.* New Brunswick, NJ: Rutgers University Press, 2003.

Dale, Frank. *Delaware Diary: Episodes in the Life of a River.* New Brunswick, NJ: Rutgers University Press, 1996.

Decker, Amelia Stickney. *That Ancient Trail: The Old Mine Road.* Trenton, NJ: Petty Printing, 1942.

Dorfinger, Don and Marietta. *River Towns of the Delaware Water Gap.* Charleston, SC: Arcadia Publishing, 2017.

Gladowski, Michael P. *Delaware Water Gap National Recreation Area.* Atglen, PA: Schiffer Publishing, 2019.

Groth, Charlie. *Another Haul: Narrative Stewardship and Cultural Sustainability at the Lewis Family Fishery.* Jackson: University Press of Mississippi, 2019.

Hine, C.G. *The Old Mine Road.* New Brunswick, NJ: Rutgers University Press, 1963.

Lee, James. *The Morris Canal: A Photographic History*. Easton: Delaware Press, 1973.

Lee, Laura M., and Brendan Mackie. *Fort Delaware*. Charleston, SC: Arcadia Publishing, 2010.

Lurie, Maxine, and Peter Wacker, eds. *Mapping New Jersey*. New Brunswick, NJ: Rutgers University Press, 2017.

Menzies, Elizabeth. *Passage between Rivers: A Portfolio of Photographs with a History of the Delaware and Raritan Canal*. New Brunswick, NJ: Rutgers University Press, 1976.

Moyer, Frank Harris. *The Delaware River: History, Tradition & Legends*. Charleston, SC: The History Press), 2019

Obiso, Laura. *Delaware Water Gap National Recreation Area*. Charleston, SC: Arcadia Publishing, 2009.

Safian, Gail F. *Slavery in New Jersey: A Troubled History*. Maplewood, NJ: Durando-Hedden House, 2019.

Richman, Steven M. *The Bridges of New Jersey: Portraits of Garden State Crossings*. New Brunswick, NJ: Rutgers University Press, 2005.

Rockland, Michael Aaron. *The George Washington Bridge: Poetry in Steel*. Revised and expanded ed. New Brunswick, NJ: Rutgers University Press, 2020.

Stroud, Patricia Tyson. *The Man Who Had Been King: The American Exile of Napoleon's Brother Joseph*. Philadelphia: University of Pennsylvania Press, 2005.

Stutz, Bruce. *Natural Lives: People and Places of the Delaware River*. New York: Crown, 1992.

Veit, Richard F. *The Old Canals of New Jersey*. Little Falls: New Jersey Geographical Press, 1963.

Works Progress Administration. *Stories of New Jersey*. New York: M. Barrows and Co., 1938.

Index

Bonaparte, Joseph, 6, 120; houses of, 116, 117–119; Spain fled by, 114, 115–116; staircase of, 111, 112; tunnels of, 111, 113; visitors of, 119
Bonaparte, Napoleon, 114, 115
bookstore, Frenchtown, 97
Bordentown: Bonaparte, J., stay in, 116; D&R section in, 82, 83
Bray, Daniel, 96; Durham boats gathered by, 106; Highway named after, 88, 106
bridges, 24, 26, 121; for Bonaparte, J., 111, 113; covered, 59–60, 123–125; for D&R recreational pathway, 85–86; pedestrian, 125–127; swing, 80; toll, 122, 128; wire suspension and narrow, 130. *See also specific bridges*
bridgetender houses, 80
Bridgeton, New Jersey, 141
British Army, 23, 106–108
Bryant, William Cullen, 6
Bull's Island, New Jersey, 80, 81, 94–95
Burlington, New Jersey, 32–34
Burlington County Historical Society, 33
Burlington Island, New Jersey, 24, 29, 33; debris on, 30, 31; Dutch settlers on, 30, 32; lake within, 34–35; resort on, 30
Buttermilk Falls, New Jersey, 47
Byrne, Brendan, 64–65

cabins, on Burlington Island, 30
cacti, 7, 8
Camden, New Jersey, 29
Canal Society of New Jersey, 79
canoeing, through Delaware Water Gap, 45
Cape May, New Jersey, 14–15, 16, 136, 138
Carluccio, Tracy, 63
carnival, in Lambertville, 90
Carter, Jimmy, 67
Carteret, George, 14
Carver, George Washington, 105
caviar, from Bayside, 136
cemeteries: Confederate prisoner mass graves, 40; for Delaware and Raritan Canal laborers, 81; Frenchtown superintendent of, 99; for veterans, 42. *See also* Finn's Point, New Jersey
Centre Bridge, 123
Chesapeake and Delaware Canal, 36–37, 84

cholera epidemic, 81
Civil War, 103; Andersonville prison during, 38–39; Fort Delaware prison during, 37, 38, 39; slavery during, 133
climate change, sea level rise from, 140
Coca-Cola, covered bridge advertisement of, 124
Cole, Thomas, 5, 6
Colescott, Robert, 105
Colligan's Stockton Inn, in Stockton, 91–92
Colorado River, 59
community: gay, 89; of Lewis Island, 27
Confederacy, 37, 41, 133
Confederate prisoners: Finn's Point monument for, 40–41; at Fort Delaware, 37, 38, 39; mass graves of, 40
Connelly, Owen. See *Gentle Bonaparte, The*
Constitution, U.S., 37–38
Continental Army, 56, 105
Coombs, Ben, 98
Cooper, James Fenimore, 33
corpses, state jurisdiction of, 20
covered bridges, 125; advertisements on, 124; floods destroying, 59–60, 123–124
Crosswicks Creek, New Jersey, 111
Cumberland County, New Jersey, 133, 139, 141
Cunanan, Andrew, 42–43

dams: building trends of, 68, 69, 70; Hoover Dam, 59, 69; mini, 81, 94–95; Sewell Bluff Dam, 67; Teton Dam, 63. *See also* Tocks Island Dam, New Jersey
Daniel Bray Highway, New Jersey, 88, 106
deaths: from Delaware Bay tsunami, 132; from hurricanes, 61
Deer Head Inn (Delaware Water Gap, Pennsylvania), 51
Delaware: New Jersey border with, 18, 20–21; Pea Patch Island, 24, 35–43
Delaware and Raritan Canal (1834) (D&R Canal), 71–72, 73, 78; feeder, 80–81, 82, 85, 86, 94–96; laborers for, 80–81; locks of, 82; recreational pathway along, 79, 80, 84, 85–86, 96–97; State Park, 64, 84–85, 93, 95; during WWII, 83
Delaware and Raritan Greenway Land Trust, 118

About the Author

MICHAEL AARON ROCKLAND is an emeritus professor of American studies at Rutgers University and the author of some fifteen books, several published with Rutgers University Press. Equally drawn to scholarship, fiction, and memoir, two of his books were selected by the *New York Times* and the *Washington Post* for their lists of Fifty Best Books of the Year. A book he co-wrote was chosen by the New Jersey State Library as one of the ten best books ever written about New Jersey or by a New Jerseyan. Among his awards as a professor, he won his university's scholar-teacher award and the national teaching award in American studies. Besides his books he has written over sixty feature stories, mostly for the state magazine *New Jersey Monthly*, which contributed to his receiving the Governor Richard J. Hughes Award for "a lifetime of contributions to New Jersey history and culture." Prior to his academic and writing career, he served in the United States diplomatic service as a cultural attaché with the American embassies in Argentina and in Spain, and has continued his international involvement over the years by receiving four Fulbright awards and lecturing in some twenty-six nations.